WHEN "EYE" WOKE UP

*My bad habits
led me to the light
and I changed my reality.*

TIMOTHY MAHAN

Text: Timothy Mahan
Editor: Rachel Small
Cover Design: David Tafolla
Interior Design & Layout: Danielle Smith-Boldt

ISBN: 979-8-218-12380-2

Disclaimer: All events and actions described in this book
are my own experience. I used common sense with trial
and error to find my way. Everyone's situation is different.
Don't cleanse your body or change your diet without
consulting your doctor first. What worked for me might not
work for you.

Author's Note

If you're buying this book for help to get off prescription drugs and want to use my template, go directly to chapter six and read through chapter seven. If you're in a life threatening drug withdrawal condition, call 911 for immediate help.

Kids, I suggest that you never take any doctor prescribed pain pills, Xanax, or Adderal outside of hospital care. Going through this experience cost me everything I ever loved. I ultimately lost my business and millions in revenue.

For ten years, opioids clouded my vision, destroyed my body, and took my soul. But even when I was in their grip, I knew deep down the time would come when I'd have to get clean. And I did. Come to find out we're all self-healers, and in this book, I'll take you on a journey through my life to getting clean and healing my physical body. I want you to know that once you commit to your health, the Universe, or God, or whatever you call your higher power will start to remove people from your life and help you in ways that you could never imagine. "This book is meant to serve as a beacon of hope for you or a loved one."

If you're tired of living a life of struggle, and are looking for a way to access joy, this book is for you. We create our own hell and our own heaven from within, and my story is proof of this.

If you or a loved one is struggling with prescribed medication, this book is for you. As a husband, father, and business owner, I had the world at my fingertips. I had to let go of everything for a season in my life to overcome my deadly addiction.

If you're a doctor, or dentist who has the power to write prescriptions, this book is for you. I hope that through my story, you'll gain a better understanding of just how much these pills can affect someone's life.

If you're a parent, this book is for you. Kids are born as loving energy programmed perfectly to change the world. However, they are programmed into the world we live in through observing their environment, and us the parents. Do we want our kids to be mirror images of us, or do we want them to be better than us?

If you're looking for a different perspective on who we are, then this book is for you. During my life changing transformation from being stuck on doctor prescribed medication to becoming the joyful person I am today-I picked up knowledge. When I shed my old skin, the world opened up to me. As I changed, the world I used to perceive started to change. I've now come to the realization that we're all one with separate personalities collectively vibrating and manifesting the world we live in by how we feel, our thoughts and actions. What I mean by oneness is this, we're all incubated and born the same way through a woman. We're nothing more than flesh and bones until we take our first breath. This is when we invite our spirit into our pure bodies. We develop our own personality or avatars based on the environment and upbringing we grow up in. I like to think of it like this, we're a bunch of ants connected or disconnected from each other based on our lifestyle and beliefs. Once we change our life style and our beliefs, we disconnect from the old group and connect with a new group that have the same mindset. You can level up, or level down based on your perception of yourself.

In the final chapter, "How I Healed Myself." I will take you through the process of how I got clean and how I dropped forty-five pounds in under three months. Once you commit to changing your life for the better, there's no going back. Choose your friends and environment wisely. You may have to let go of people who are no longer on your wave length, or frequency. It doesn't mean you're better than anyone. It simply means you're moving into a state of higher vibration or consciousness. You're changing for the better. Time to level up!

Table of Contents

Introduction

Your mind is the Garden of Eden.
Seed it wisely.

I don't know if anyone reading this book believes in spirits, or energy, but after going through my healing experience, I've come to realize that there is more to this world than the human eye can see.

What if the world was just a mirror showing you who you are through other people and experiences? What if our childhood programming created your life un knowingly, and in order to re-create yourself, you must disconnect from your old life and connect to one you truly want to live? Maybe, I can answer some of these questions throughout this book and connect the dots to gain a better understanding about how I got addicted to these pills. I believe there's definitely a force above helping us achieve the life of our dreams. The good and the bad.

Here's an old wise tale describing how we're always being guided to the place we choose to be.

The biblical version of the Three Wise Men resonated with me when I first read it. Then out of nowhere I saw a short YouTube video about the three wise men describing this story as energy. I'm going to tell my version of the story using the term spirits.

Once, there were three wise men. One carried the spirit of love, one carried the spirit of prosperity, and one carried the spirit of wisdom. These men visited a town to bless a couple expecting a baby. When the wise men arrived at the couple's house, Love knocked on the door.

A woman answered, "May I help you?"

Love said, "Yes, is your husband home?"

The lady responded, "He's not home, but he'll be home at 5:00 p.m., when he gets off work. You can wait inside for him if you'd like."

"We cannot come into your home until your husband is here. Do you mind if we wait outside?" Love asked.

The woman agreed. When her husband arrived home, he came to the door and asked the wise men, "How may I help you?"

Love said, "You're about to have a baby, so we're here to bless your home with love, prosperity, or wisdom, but you can only pick one blessing."

The couple stepped back to discuss their choice. The husband wanted prosperity. He said, "hunny, do you know what we could do with all of this money?" The wife in a calm manner looked him in his eyes, and softly said, "What's the point of having all that prosperity with no love in your home? Choose love."

While looking into his wife's eyes, a loving vibration came over him, and his heart started to open up. The husband never truly felt this feeling before, and he liked it. As he started to relax, he leaned down to kiss his wife and then with a huge smile on his face, he agreed, "Lets choose love."

They returned to the front door, where the wise men stood, and said, "We choose to have our home blessed with love."

All three wise men looked at each other smiling ear to ear and said, "That's a wise decision young man. Since you chose love, we will bless your house with all three spirits. As long as you hold the vibration of love in your heart and do everything with love, you'll always be blessed."

The wife and husband were so happy. Shortly after the wise men's visit, the wife gave birth to a baby boy. The husband quit his job and started his own construction company. The business soon took off, and the family moved into a new, bigger home. Life seemed to be moving in a positive direction as the blessings of prosperity started to come, but the husband lacked wisdom.

Two years later, the wife gave birth to a baby girl. By this point, the husband was making good money through his business, but he'd become addicted to pain pills. Neither he nor his wife saw this coming. Who could have known the pills would close his heart. As his heart closed, he lost his loving spirit and then his ego began taking over his life. Shortly after, he started drinking at bars after work. Now he's bringing home new negative spirits he picked up from his new activity that didn't belong in his house.

Four years after their first visit, the three wise men returned. This time, when Love knocked on the door, the husband answered. The three wise men asked if the wife was home. The husband said, "She's not home, but since I'm the head of the household, I make all of the decisions now."

Looking puzzled, the three wise men asked the husband which blessing he'd like for their home, and he quickly replied, "Prosperity." All three wise men looked at each other confused, and blessed the home with prosperity.

Over the following months, the husband's business shot through the roof. The family again moved into a larger home. They also bought a couple of new vehicles, and the husband got a new office. But the husband started to stretch himself too thin and started to bring home the spirit of stress and frustration. The family started to experience unnecessary growing pains and the husband began taking more pills which affected both his home and business life.

Four years after the wise men's second visit, only one wise man visited the couple's new home this time. It was the spirit of Wisdom. When Wisdom knocked on the door, both the husband and wife answered. (HELP) "I can't stand this guy anymore, I want a separation," said the wife. "I just want off of these pills, their killing me," said the husband.

Wisdom smiled and said, "Don't worry, I've been with you all along. Help is on the way."

After Wisdom's visit, the husband was visited by the cannabis spirit to give him the medicine he would need to get through the withdrawals a few months down the line. The husband said, "I don't touch that stuff," but accepted the medicine and put it in his dresser drawer at home. A month later, he was electrocuted, and two weeks after that, he was bit by a spider and on the way home, hit by a truck. He then eventually fell from a building and fractured his ankle which rendered him unable to perform at work. The husband started to lose his money, which prevented him from buying prescription pills.

The energy of wisdom wasn't finished with the husband yet. Wisdom used the husband's ego to get him out of the country so he could detox, heal, and envision a new future for himself.

When he returned home, the husband lost his energetic connection to his business, his wife, and his kids so he could learn humility. He then lost his house and became homeless so he could learn gratitude. He was also being shown where his experience and talents can help others.

Wisdom still wasn't finished with the husband yet. It was time to bless his wife with the separation she wanted, and she was gifted with new love, in the form of a younger man. The husband was mad at first, but he soon realized that both he and his wife were being blessed with the freedom they needed, and he thanked Love for returning to his family's life.

Wisdom left the husband with the knowledge he needed to move forward on a better foundation. And after a long journey to healing, he realized he'd received what he asked for, just not in the way that he'd asked for it. He learned how to light up his own world through purification of his mind and body. This is my story!

PART ONE

GROWING UP

CHAPTER ONE
The Beginning

My family wasn't always broken. It broke when drugs and alcohol infiltrated us.

I grew up in the city of San Bernardino, in Southern California. The city is located at the bottom of the San Bernardino mountains off highway 18. This was once a military town known for being a safe place to raise a family with lots of local businesses. Today, San Bernardino is known as a poor city filled with crime and violence. This town has become commercialized with corporations and government agencies.

We moved around a lot and didn't have much money. As a kid, I didn't know why my mom and dad fought all the time, but I observed a lot of violence and anger.

Both of my parents lived in a low energetic vibration I now call hell. My mom always seemed to be upset, and she radiated negative energy. I could always feel this energy in the house, and it scared me. My dad was hardly home, but when he was home, my mom and him were always fighting. This would scare the shit out of me.

In hindsight, I'm thankful I grew up this way. My upbringing served as an example of what I didn't want in life. I didn't want to be poor. I didn't want to live a life full of anger and violence. I promised myself I'd do anything to give my kids a better life than I had growing up.

My dad was a big man with a loud voice and a big heart. When I was a child, I saw him as superman. It wasn't until I got older that I understood the things he'd done were wrong. But before he passed over into the spiritual realm, in October 2013, from brain cancer, he became a changed man. He was a wonderful grandpa to my kids and my step sister's kids. He treated them like kings and queens. I'm thankful they saw the best in him. I loved my dad.

Today, my mom and I have a better relationship. We're able to talk without arguing. She treats my kids better than she treated my brother and me growing up. Another blessing! I'm thankful my kids have seen the best side of her. I love my mom.

Despite growing up in the same household, my brother and I turned out very differently. Without saying who was "good" and who was "bad," let's just say we took different paths to wind up on the same road. I also have two half-brothers from my dad's side. I love my brothers.

Now that I'm forty, my childhood is mostly a blur, but I do remember vowing I'd never use cigarettes, drugs, or alcohol because the substances contributed to the death of my entire family on my dad's side. The drugs, coupled with bad diets, created cancer, heart attacks, and brain aneurysms.

Despite the negative environment I lived in, I also learned some good habits from my parents, such as how to work hard, and pay bills in this world. There's always a positive along with a negative. I don't hold anything against my parents. They did the best that they knew how. They were once children growing up watching their parents, and they probably had it even worse. That's how the cycle of life works, each generation is supposed to become better human beans than the last, but some families take longer than others to level up because the children don't learn from their parents' mistakes.

There is no instruction manual for this life. Some people may argue that the Bible is the instruction manual. I have read the Bible multiple times. This book speaks a lot of spiritual wisdom. Come to find out, the Bible is the world's greatest healing book. As I'd come to realize after all of these years, living life is the greatest teacher of all.

My Introduction to Drugs

This will go against conventional wisdom, but at a young age I was given my first drug in the form of sugar. I don't remember who introduced the candy to me, but I loved the taste. This drug was easy to get once I got addicted to it. Every drug store, gas station, and liquor store had my goods on the bottom shelf next to the cash register.

From there, I started to drink Pepsi with my hamburgers and pizza. To this day, I must have a Pepsi with my pizza. I don't feel very good after I indulge in these foods, so I have cut them out of my diet for the most part. Who would have known that the largest drug manufacturers in the world are the corporations that make these products. They use gas stations, liquor stores, and grocery stores to deal their goods to our kids.

When I was fourteen, my friends and I decided to have some fun with a plant we named Trippy root. One of my friends said that the plant made him hallucinate, so five of us walked to the wash and dug the plant up by its roots. We took the roots back to my friend's house and boiled them in water. We then added tea for flavor and filled up a 2-gallon Gatorade jug with the brew we called Trippy tea. We drank the entire jug and proceeded to go on a spiritual trip probably fifty times stronger than acid. We could see behind the veil of this world.

We hallucinated for a week. I remember seeing my dogs even though they were physically forty miles away. We all spoke a different language that sounded like baby talk. We understood what we were talking about, but our parents couldn't.

My brother and I would get up and run head first into the walls as if they didn't exist. I remember feeling as though we'd brought our spirits into the physical realm through our bodies, and the spirits didn't know what to do. We were in another dimension or something. Our parents had to lock all the doors and barricade us in the living room. They were afraid that we were going to leave the house and get hit by a car. On day five of my spiritual trip, I remember going partially blind for a short amount of time.

When I look back on this experience after all of these years, I come to realize that there's more to us as humans than we realize. This plant opened me up to something more than my imagination. I've always wondered what we could learn from this plant in a controlled environment drinking a lot less than we did, but I'm way too afraid to ever try it again.

When I was 16, I needed to have my wisdom teeth extracted. I was knocked out with anesthesia during the surgery and afterward, my mouth was extremely swollen and sore. The dentist prescribed me Vicodin for the pain. This was my first taste of an opiate, and I absolutely loved the feeling. The Vicodin did more than numb the pain. It turned off the thoughts in my mind that were no good. I felt happy and energetic. I remember thinking, "If these pills come from a doctor, they must be safe!"

Thankfully, after my prescription ran out, I didn't have any desire to take any more pills. I forgot about the feeling and moved on with my life.

My Second Encounter with Vicodin

In June 2004, when I was 23 years old, my girlfriend (who would later become my wife) and I took a trip to Las Vegas. I loved her more than anything else in the world at the time. I would have done anything for her. I would have fought to the death to protect her from any outside forces. We were young and in love.

In a casino on the strip, we walked past a guy who started to say some inappropriate things to my girlfriend. I turned around and told him to shut up and suddenly, two other guys ran up behind me and started punching me. Both of the guys ended up falling on the ground somehow and I jumped on one of the guys and started returning the favor.

The casino's security team rushed in to break up the altercation. They grabbed my right arm as I was throwing a punch, tearing my rotator cuff. Then, when they were handcuffing me, they yanked my right arm behind my back and pulled it to the top of my head, dislocating my right shoulder. I'd injured this shoulder in my teenage years, when I got my arm stuck in an electric gate.

The security team took us to a room in the back of the casino, they told me to sit down on some stairs, and then handcuffed me to a handrail with my arms above my head. The other three guys were placed in a room to fill out paperwork. It felt as if we were there for hours. I lost track of time. I remember being in a lot of pain.

We were finally released at 3:00 a.m. While my girlfriend and I were walking to our room, I was able to put my shoulder back into place but I was still in a lot of pain. Looking back, if I was never drinking, I would have never lowered my vibrational frequency to attract this incident into my life. In a weird way, I must have been broadcasting an aggressive vibration, or she was broadcasting a seductive vibration. This is why alcohol is not good for me to consume in high volumes.

The Monday after our trip, I was in so much pain I could not go to work. I went to the hospital but I didn't have insurance at the time, so I couldn't afford surgery. I explained to the doctor that I was a steel framer and I hung drywall for a living. She gave me a note that stated I should take two weeks off work. I also asked if she could prescribe me some pills for the pain. And she did: ninety 5-mg Vicodin pills to take for the next three months. I took only one per day, as per the directions. Once the three months were up, I was still in a lot of pain and I noticed that while I was on the medication, I had little regard for the pain. I went back to my doctor and she gave me a prescription for an additional three months.

I loved the pills. They numbed the pain and allowed me to get through each day without a care in the world, full of energy. Once the six months were up, the doctor cut me off, but I didn't notice any withdrawal symptoms, or discomfort. This was when I got the idea into my head that these pills weren't dangerous. (Man), I had no idea how much pain I was going to go through thirteen years later.

My Lessons Begin

In 2005, my girlfriend got pregnant. Full of love and ready to take on the world, we decided to get married. At the time, I was a sixth stage Union Steel Framer. I was tired of working for a company and wanted to start my own. I also wanted to make more money so my wife could stay at home to raise our son. I wanted to give him a better upbringing than I had since I didn't have a mom at home to raise me. She was always gone at work.

Thankfully, the Universe lined up an event that was able to move me into the right direction. While at work one day, I was framing walls when my brother, who worked for the same company, tripped over some steel studs. The foreman belittled him in front of the crew. Hearing this, I came down from the scissor lift to confront the foreman about disrespecting my brother. After a brief argument, I left the job-site. When I returned the next day, the energy didn't seem right. I felt as if I didn't belong on the job site any longer.

I ended up quitting my job with two hundred dollars in my pocket and I went on to start a drywall company with my brothers help. Between 2005 and 2007, The business grew exponentially. I was meeting the right people at the right time, and our lives were great. We moved into a new home and started living the American dream. But once I started making money, I started to drink more often. I felt like drinking was what adults did after work. I always saw adults drinking while growing up. Every night after work, I'd come home, take a shot of vodka, and then sit on the couch to watch TV while drinking beer. It became a routine. Who knew drinking was weakening my vibration to allow lower vibrational energy in the form of people into my life.

In 2007, I linked up with an old friend from elementary school, he was an up-and-coming tattoo artist in Southern California. His tattoos were nothing like anyone had seen before at that time. Growing up, he was like a big brother to me. I was one of the smallest kids at school and for some reason, I always had a bully messing with me. He used to come to my rescue and beat up the bigger kids.

He was in need of someone to expand his tattoo shop, so we worked out a barter. I'd expand his shop, and he'd provide the materials as well as tattoo me. I wanted a dragon going over my shoulder, but he had a better plan. He had a vision of tattooing the dragon over my entire back.

Several months before my tattoo session, a friend got into a car accident. He refused to take any of the pain pills he'd been prescribed, saying that he hated taking pills. I asked him if I could have them for my tattoo session. He said no problem, and gave them to me. Who would have known this was the start of the biggest life lesson I would ever learn in this world?

My back tattoo took thirteen months to complete. I started out taking two Vicodin pills a session. They didn't mask the pain they just helped me not care. This where I started to mess up. The pills made me feel like Superman. When I took them, I had greater focus and energy at work. I was able to accomplish more than my competitor at a cheaper price. Once people heard I was good at my craft, and cheap, my calendar filled up quick. Since I was growing exponentially, I started to bring on growing pains. I took on too much work at a fraction of my competitor's price. I was overworked and underpaid. And it ended up costing me the best years with my children. I was never home to ever be a real father. When I wasn't working, I was either sick, sleeping, or on the phone. I'm grateful for my wife's ability to endure those years.

Between 2007 and 2010, I went from taking two 5-mg Vicodin pills a day to ten 10-mg Norco pills a day. During those years, Norco's were easy to get. It seemed as if they were all around me, and everyone I knew was taking them. But near the end of 2010, my connection lost their prescription. And I soon started to feel sick. This was my first time experiencing withdrawal symptoms, and I had no idea what was happening to me. I had chest pain that was so bad that I thought I was going to have a heart attack. I felt weak and tired. I also became irritable, which was out of my character.

I went to the ER and told the doctor, "I've been taking ten Norcos a day, and I drink beer every day after work. Now I'm sick."

"You just have anxiety," the doctor replied. "Ten Norcos a day isn't that bad."

The comment made me feel a little better mentally, but it didn't fix my chest pain. He then gave me a little white pill named Ativan. In about twenty minutes, the pain went away and I'd calmed down. It was as if the doctor had given me a miracle pill. He then gave me a prescription for ten and recommended that I followed up with my doctor to figure out how I could manage my chest pain, but I didn't follow up with my doctor.

Now, I had my new miracle new drug, and I also ended up finding a new Norco connection from friends of friends, along with two new pills: 30-mg Roxicodone and 30-mg extended-release OxyContin. These pills didn't stay in my experience very long, that's for sure.

The first Roxicodone I ever took knocked me on my ass. I normally took 100-mgs of hydrocodone (Norco) per day. Not knowing the chemical make-up of a Norco was different from that of a Roxicodone, I took one Roxicodone with two Norco's on my way to work one day. Behind the wheel, I started to feel really tired and itchy. *"What the hell kind of pill is this?"* Immediately after pulling up to the job site, I found a quiet room and passed out. After that experience, I kept the Roxicodone and OxyContin for emergencies only, and only for two years. The pills prevented me from working at my maximum potential. Well, the maximum potential the Norcos allowed me to work, if I wasn't going through withdrawals.

I'd still experience chest pain when I didn't take enough Norcos during the day, so I started taking half a pill of Ativan to help. When I told my dad that I was taking Ativan. He said he'd been prescribed Xanax and that he liked it better than Ativan. Between 2010 and 2014, I struggled with Norco and now Xanax. I wanted to get off of these pills so badly, but I felt like I carried the world on my shoulders. I came from a poor environment, and I always seemed to be helping somebody other than myself.

In 2015, I started out having a great year financially in fact, I felt as if we were about to have our most profitable year in business ever, and I was so excited. A profitable year would give me the stability to scale back my business and finally start my recovery. Not only was I struggling with the pill abuse, but my physical body was overweight and breaking down. I had a terrible diet outside of my home. I lived such a fast-paced life, I ate fast food along with candy, Red Bull's, and soda to compliment my pill use. Knowing what I know now about the sugar in these products, I wasn't doing myself any favors.

In June of 2015, I went to put gas in my truck and my card was declined. *"Were doing great this year. What could be going on?"* As it turned out, the IRS, took all of my money. Now, I'm back in stress mode, and irate. My plans of getting clean went out the window. I had four huge projects to complete and no money in the bank. This was when I started working more hours than I could keep track of to get my projects completed. My pill use went up as a result!

I found a doctor who would prescribe me 120-Norcos and 60-Xanax bars a month. I'd go through the Norcos in about ten days. Taking close to three hundred Norcos a month now, I wanted to quit these pills so badly. I knew they were killing me slowly. If I didn't have my Norcos, I couldn't get out of bed. And my chest was always tight, so I took the Xanax in the hopes of balancing out my body.

By 2016, the combination of Norcos and Xanax wasn't quite moving me as they had in the past. I desperately wanted to quit but didn't feel financially able to. I was trying to catch up with my losses, but I was just spinning my wheels. To get clean, I'd have to shut down my company, and that would affect many people in my life. The weight on my shoulders was beyond heavy. I didn't know what to do. I needed help and didn't know how to ask for it. I was always the one helping others, now how do I ask?

Then I talked with a friend who'd been prescribed Adderall for ADHD. He said the pills helped him focus and gave him energy. *Bingo*, that's what I needed, more energy. If I could just contract more work, and make more money, surely I'd be able to buy time and get clean. Boy was I wrong. It made matters worse. I was too busy, and I was losing touch with who I was. After asking a doctor for an Adderall prescription and being refused, I found some on the street through friends, and began taking Adderall combined with Norcos. I also continued using Xanax to reduce my chest pain. When I started taking Adderall, I couldn't sleep at night, so I started taking more Xanax than usual for sleep.

This brought my daily pill cocktail to around fifteen Norcos, four bars of Xanax, and three Adderall pills. I was ashamed, unhappy, and losing touch with myself. All I could think was, "How could this have happened to me?"

CHAPTER TWO

Wake-Up Call

"I was in need of healing from opioid addiction. I asked the universe to help me clean up my life. Soon after I asked for help, it arrived in the form of cannabis, unexpectedly. After a near death experience in terrible pain, I tried the plant instead of taking pain pills. My life forever changed in that moment. As my spirit left my body, I was shown (My) truth, and then I was shown how the world worked. That's when I started my journey to become an awakened spirit!"

In this chapter, I will describe the events that led to my healing journey. The truth is, when my body started to die, my world started to collapse. Thank God I recognized the signs before it was too late.

My New Year's resolution going into 2017 was to quit the pills. I wanted to feel healthy. I was yearning for a day where I felt normal. At this point, I didn't even know what "normal" was anymore. My body was beaten up from all my injuries from hanging drywall, and I felt as if I were constantly in withdrawal mode. I had to put on a mask every day with my clients as if everything was fine in my life, but in actuality I was suffering on the inside.

In the early months of that year, I had a knowing it was time for me to quit these pills. I was constantly woken up at night by a dark shadow. It would wake me up and put my body in a state of paralysis, sit on me, and try to suffocate me. In order to get this dark energy off of me, I'd remain calm and fight it with my mind. I wasn't going to pass over into the spiritual realm in my sleep and leave my kids on this earth without me. No way was I going to give up my life on earth that easily. *This dark energy better bring a fucking army to take my soul.*

This continued for the better part of the year. I felt as if I had a death wish hanging over my head spiritually. I think my body was about to die from the pills, and the shadow was here to take my soul peacefully in my sleep. Then people would have said that I died in my sleep.

One morning that summer, unable to find time to just rest and be at peace, I stood in the shower crying while the water run down my head. Ever since I'd gotten hooked on the pills, I felt as if I'd been in a prison without bars. And although my family was always next to me, I always felt alone.

While in the shower, I said, "God, Jesus, Universe, if you are real, listen to me. I'm tired of these pills. I am tired of all the stress. Please, help me clean up my life. I can't do this anymore." When I said this prayer, I was full of emotion, crying my eyes out.

An Electrifying Experience 480-Volts

About month later, I met a couple cannabis cultivators that liked my work. We had a meeting about building materials for their cultivation facility. As a gift, they gave me a bunch of cannabis samples. I remember saying at the time, "I don't smoke weed, no thanks." They kinda looked at each other puzzled, but I ended up accepting the samples anyways. I put the samples in my dresser drawer at home and forgot about them. I didn't know the universe was bringing me the medicine I would need to get off of the pills ahead of time. My prayer was about to be answered on my next project, but not in the way I would have expected.

Looking back, this meeting had nothing to do with business. The Universe had delivered the medicine I'd need to get through the withdrawals I was going to experience a few months down the line.

I showed up to one of my projects around 11:00 a.m. in late September 2017 while the guys were demolishing a ceiling. I looked up and saw the main feed electrical pull box panel door open. "Who opened that pull box?" I asked. No one knew, so I asked them to stop working so

I could shut the panel door. I climbed a ladder, got on top of the ceiling, and made my way to the pull box.

And as I shut the door, a jolt of electricity shot through my body.

I was blown back approximately ten feet. I don't know how long I was unconscious. When "eye" woke up, it looked like the Fourth of July. Sparks were were flying everywhere as the wire ark'ed to the metal. I didn't feel like I was the same person anymore. I was confused, and I felt like my entire life was a dream full of lessons. I felt as if the world wasn't real anymore. I didn't want to do anything but sleep.

All the guys who'd witnessed the incident were worried about me. They urged me to go to the hospital, but I kept telling them I was fine. I just needed to sleep. *This was my wake-up call*. If I wasn't on those pills, I would have been in my right mind and I would have had an electrician close and locked out that panel.

Two weeks after the I was electrocuted in the middle of October 2017, I arrived to one of my project sites late in the afternoon. There was only one person still working. I took my daily cocktail of pills and then told my guy to go home because I was going to work all night and I needed him there in the morning. He reluctantly went home. Around 2:00 a.m., I was on a scissor lift doing some ceiling work and I felt a little pinch on the back of my leg, behind my knee. When I scratched the area, I felt something crunch between my finger and my leg. I looked and saw a brown colored spider stuck to my finger. I wiped off my finger, paid no attention to it, and continued to work.

Around 6:00 a.m., I started to feel sick. I didn't think I was experiencing withdrawal symptoms–this feeling was brand new. I started sweating profusely and I got extremely dizzy. Feeling nauseous, I ran to the restroom to throw up. As I was throwing up, I felt diarrhea coming, so I had to shift gears to make sure I didn't shit my pants. That was the last thing I remembered before I passed out. I woke up on the restroom floor about forty-five minutes later in a pool of sweat. I quickly cleaned myself up and left without telling anyone from the morning crew that I was going home.

On my way home, in my company flatbed truck, a Ford F-150 rear ended me on the freeway. Lets just say, I wasn't having a very good day. I remember thinking, *"In the last month, I've been electrocuted, bitten by a spider, and now rear-ended. What else could go wrong? Why me? What have I done to deserve this?"*

When I got home, my wife asked where I have been. I was sick as usual, but this time, The sickness from the spider bite and I'm starting to withdrawal from the pills. I told her, "I just need to get to bed." I slept for two days while my wife handled all of my phone calls. Finally, my wife woke me up for an important call. When I got off the phone, she asked what was wrong with me. I hadn't told her about the spider bite, I just mentioned I felt sick and needed to be in bed.

I asked her to look at the back of my leg. I was in a lot of pain. I remember my wife saying, "What the hell is this? There is a huge puss pocket, what happened? You need to go to the hospital!"

I told her, "I don't want to go. I'm over these pills, and the doctors are just going to give me more." So I asked her to get a knife to cut the pocket and squeeze out the pus. Thankfully, she found some suction cups, which we used to drain the fluid from the spider bite.

I slept for one more day, and started to seriously think about quitting my company to get myself healed. There were just too many incidents happening in a short amount of time. My body was beat up. My hands were always numb, and the tension in my neck was unbearable. The Universe or God was sending me a message to sit down. I should have listened after the electrocution, but staying down wasn't in my vocabulary.

Turning to Cannabis

A week before Thanksgiving, I got a phone call from a cannabis consultant to look at a building in California. The consultant had a client that wanted to do a tenant improvement project for a cultivation company. I didn't like the energy of the building. It felt heavy like there was a negative presence.

When we finished our walkthrough, and exited the building, the consultant locked the storefront door. As she started pulling down the roll-up door, the chain jumped off the sprocket and got stuck about three feet off the ground. I'd never seen this happen before.

The consultant said she'd climb up the side of the wall and put the chain back on the sprocket. "No, no," I said, "If anything were to happen, I'd prefer it happen to me!" I set down a glass Starbucks bottle I was holding, and proceeded to climb the wall using the roll- up door as a foot hold. When I was about four feet off the ground, the chain dislodged and the door came down. I jumped back toward the ground, forgetting about the bottle I just placed on the ground. My left foot landed on top of the bottle, and bottle fell over as I landed on it. As my foot hit the ground, I rolled my ankle, and I collapsed to the ground in a lot of pain. This was the last straw.

I threw up my hands and screamed, "WHAT THE HELL DO YOU WANT FROM ME!" As I lay on the ground screaming in pain. This injury nearly threw me in shock as I was sweating profusely. This time, I went to the hospital.

By the time I got to the ER, I was drenched in sweat. The pills I'd taken that morning, before my meeting, were starting to wear off. The doctor examined my X-ray, and told me, "I can't tell if your ankle is separated or broken. You definitely have a small fracture. You'll need surgery, and eight to twelve weeks to heal."

Before I could process this information, a nurse comes in the room and rolled up my left sleeve. I looked at her, and asked her. "What are you doing with that needle in your hand?"

She said, "Look at your ankle, aren't you in a lot of pain? This is morphine to relieve the pain."

"I've been trying to quit pain killers since 2010," I said. "You guys always offer me pain killers when I get hurt. I'll pass. I don't want any more pills or shots from you. I'm *done* with doctors. I'll heal myself."

My god, the last three months had been the hardest of my entire life. I needed to change, but how would I do it? How would I deal with the pain of my injuries without pills? And how would I deal with the withdrawals? I needed a plan. I ended up going home after I left the hospital reflecting on how I got to this point in time. Thanksgiving was just around the corner and I wasn't feeling very good.

That night, I was in bed with my foot in a soft cast. Both of my legs were cramping from withdrawals and I was irritable, restless, and sweating. I was so exhausted, but couldn't sleep. Suddenly, I remembered the cannabis cultivators that gave me a bunch of samples I put in my dresser drawer. I've tried smoking cannabis once when I was a kid and it scared the hell out of me. I never thought I would use this plant to heal myself, but, "What do I have to lose?"

Well, in actuality, I had everything to lose. I had a wife, two kids, a dog, a cat, a house, three cars, two offices, and a business. And if I didn't heal myself, I'd leave this planet and lose everything through death anyways. I was stuck between a rock and a hard place. "What's my decision?" Live or die? I chose life and was willing to try anything.

So, I pulled out the cannabis from the dresser drawer. Thank God they'd given me some pre-rolled joints, but I didn't have a lighter. *Shit!* Now I had to ask my wife if she could find me one. I didn't want to tell her I was going to smoke some cannabis to feel better, but I had no choice. I wasn't in any condition to be walking around. Thankfully, my wife was all for me using the plant to relieve my pain and just relax. After all, she was living in my hell with me.

I made my way to the backyard and sat in a chair, feeling nervous. I didn't know what I was doing and I had no idea what to expect. This was strong medicine, after all. What if I smoked too much? I lit the joint and took a hit. I didn't know if I inhaled properly, so I took another hit and then put it out. I didn't feel anything right away. I got up to make my way back to the bedroom with my wife's help. As I laid down, I started to feel a numbing sensation throughout my entire body. I was starting to relax. The withdrawals didn't seem as bad, and my ankle stopped bothering me. I was falling asleep for some much needed rest.

That night, I had some of the most incredible dreams I've ever had. I hadn't dreamed in years. It seemed as if the doctor-prescribed pills had numbed everything in my brain and the cannabis was now unlocking my subconscious mind, or the world within myself. To this day, I don't know if what I saw in my dreams was real or fake. This is probably where I became mentally confused and started to chase my dreams.

In one of my dreams, I was on another earth or in a different dimension flying around with no physical body. Imagine living on earth where everything was perfect. The beauty of this planet was indescribable. My soul felt free and at peace. I felt as if I were home.

In my next dream, I was the president of the United States. I was told that I was to use my old life as a template to fix the world's problems and bring everyone together. I was able to fix all of the world's problems with my mind. If I saw a homeless man, I would envision him being rich. If I saw violence, I would envision peace. Whatever I envisioned became the current reality. I felt so powerful in this dream.

From here, I was taken to my next dream, where I was shown how our current world worked and how everything and everybody was connected based on their thought. I lived in a mind field full of negative thoughts. From birth, I was drugged and held in a lower vibration through my food, water, and air to pollute my body. The foods used were, canned vegetables, canned fruit, boxed cereal, boxed food, fake chips, processed meat, candy, soda, sports drinks, juice boxes, and chem trails.

While growing up, I was programmed to think I was free through cultural conditioning from my parents, and school system. I lived in an ego driven land with no regard for anything or anyone but myself. I was to be successful at all cost. I lived in the land of the modern slave. I was vibrationally separated from myself by race, drugs and money.

I woke up and I started to question everything in my life. Nothing seemed real to me anymore. I felt like I was living a life filled with lessons, and that everything in my life was set up for the lessons. It still remains to be seen if these dreams were showing me my past and future life, but one thing was clear: I had some healing to do.

When I opened up my spiritual gate through cannabis, I was receiving messages from the realm we cannot see, taste or touch. Are these dreams real? Is there truth to what I'm receiving? Do I really feel free? This is why cannabis is called a gateway drug. It's not a gateway to other drugs, it's the gateway to the non-physical spiritual realm. It's the gateway to see inside of yourself. I believe these were my subconscious thoughts coming to the surface in my dream state.

Cannabis really opened me up to a different level of thinking. This was the start to my healing process, but I still needed a plan. A big part of me wanted to take my pills and jump back into the everyday grind, but whenever I smoked cannabis, the urge lessened. I'd relax and find myself reflecting on life. I decided to start tapering down my pill dosages by one pill each week. It took four months to get down to a couple of pills a week. And it was definitely a process while trying to run a company. I was always sweating and low on energy. My diet didn't help matters.

By the beginning of 2018, I was taking seven to ten of Norcos, three bars of Xanax, and two Adderall pills. I was also smoking cannabis in the morning and at night, just trying to get through my days. Whenever I smoked cannabis, it would numb my entire body. I would feel tingly and relaxed. I was starting to get addicted to the feeling of feeling good all the time. *"Have I just traded in one drug for another?"* The only thing I didn't like about cannabis was that it made me feel lazy and unmotivated. I'd often times find myself daydreaming about my amazing future when I should have been focusing on keeping my business alive. But then again, what was I supposed to do? Healing is what cannabis is supposed to be used for. I was still withdrawing from pills, and every day felt like a fight for my life. The cannabis helped me through the pain. The plant was serving its purpose. It just wasn't serving my ego like the pills did.

By February, 2018. I was down to about two or three Norcos, one bar of Xanax, and half an Adderall pill per day. I wasn't feeling as tired as I usually did, though I still sweat every day and my legs were constantly cramping. All I wanted to do was sleep, but I forced myself up every day to do my rounds, going from project to project.

By mid-March, I was now smoking more cannabis than anything. I'd developed a habit of waking up to smoke a bowl and daydream before work. Cannabis was my new medicine, and I didn't know how to use it. After all, there's no instruction manual on the proper way to consume cannabis.

In May of 2018, I was almost completely off the pills feeling a lot better, but I was still sweating and had sore legs. During the five months of detoxing and healing, my body— bones, muscles, ligaments, and tendons hurt all the time. My hands were always going numb. My body was completely out of balance. I needed to finish getting off the pills. But I was also dealing with another difficult reality: my business was sinking. I hadn't been present enough over the last few months to hold everything together. The stress was mounting, and the money was running dry. Healing myself had been mentally, physically, and financially draining, and I still didn't know what "normal" felt like. *Maybe it's time to quit smoking cannabis?* It had been a great tool to get through the withdrawals, it was now time to get back to my natural state of being, whatever that looked like.

CHAPTER THREE

Connecting the Dots

"Familiarity breeds contempt. This means, if you're in an environment with the same friends doing drugs and partying, you're more than likely going to continue going around the mountain, and never grow. I learned this from receiving an unexpected invitation to China. While abroad, I had a lot of time to reflect on life. I was able to view my current life from afar. This is how I truly started to grow."

One day in late May, I was in bed scrolling through LinkedIn posts on my laptop when I came across a 3D printed concrete castle. I was so amazed, I immediately got a burst of energy. I pointed at the screen on my laptop and said, "I want this!" I then typed that comment in the message box, "I want this." I'd always wanted to build concrete homes, and with this technology, I could see the future.

Something came over me, I had a sudden burst of energy, followed by visions on how to use this equipment. I knew it wasn't the pills because by this point, I was down to half a Norco per day with no Xanax or Adderall. And it wasn't the cannabis because that made me feel relaxed. Maybe it was my ego?

Soon after I wrote the comment, "I want this," I received a direct message on my LinkedIn account from a businessman based in Brazil. "If I connect you with the CEO of the largest 3D printing company in China, will you call him?"

I said, "YES, send over the contact information!" He never did.

Then came a moment I'll never forget. On June 1, 2018, around 6:45 p.m., I was in the sauna at LA Fitness trying to cleanse my body. As soon as I got out of the sauna, my phone rang. When I looked at my phone, the phone number was unlike any phone number I have ever seen in my life.

I answered the phone, and the man on the other line said, "May I speak with Mr. Tim?"

My heart sank into my stomach, and I got very nervous. "This is Tim speaking."

"My name is John, and I'm the import and export manager for Winsun 3D. We have received an email that you are interested in our technology."

I replied, "Yes, I love the technology, and I have so many ideas on how to use it."

"Great. I would like to invite you to Shanghai, so you can visit our Research and Development Center. Please give me your email!" I started jumping up and down like a little kid. I was so excited. I wanted to build new homes from concrete, and this was the best method of achieving this goal. I didn't even think twice about my decision to go. The Universe was about to change my life, but not in the way I expected.

A day before I left for China to seek new technology, I all of a sudden lost my appetite and didn't want to eat. I was excited, but still not 100% healthy. I truly thought I was going to China for a 3D Printer to 3D print a new world. As it turns out, I was on my way to finalize my healing, and cleanse my mind from all of the bad programming I picked up from my environment in the States. I was on my way to a foreign land where I did not have access to pills or cannabis, so I thought. I was about to unknowingly learn how to take care of my body and change my life.

Travel Adventure

Feel extremely happy and energetic to move in a different direction, I lost my appetite. All I could think about was getting to Shanghai. On that big day, I arrived at LAX in Los Angeles July 4th 2018, I inserted my passport into the kiosk to get my plane ticket and it said there was no booking. A little confused, I headed to the reception desk to see why the kiosk wouldn't print my plane ticket. The woman said I didn't have a valid visa for travel to mainland China. As my heart sunk into my chest, I got a thought to change my flight to Hong Kong and apply for a visa there.

When I arrived in Hong Kong a day later, I immediately went to the immigration office to apply for my visa and I was approved for a three-day travel visa. It was now Friday in Hong Kong. My meeting with the 3D company was on Monday. That meant I could only meet with 3D company for an hour before I had to catch my plane back home.

After going through the immigration process at the airport, I booked a flight from Hong Kong to PVG airport in Pudong. I'd now been traveling for about twenty-four hours at this point. I haven't eaten much food, or drank much water and I was starting feel hungry, and dehydrated, but I didn't feel like eating. I was too busy trying to navigate myself to my destinations.

When I arrived to PVG airport around 6:00 p.m. and got off the plane, I realized I didn't have any hotel accommodations booked now that my travel plans changed. I basically parachuted into China with no plan. As I was walking down the aisle to exit the airport with hundreds of other travelers, a lady put a sign in my face that said "Four-star Chinese hotel." I shrugged her off and kept walking. She continued to follow me with the sign in my face and telling me this was the best four-star hotel in China. When I got to the end of the line, I again realized that I had no idea on how to book a hotel, so I agreed to go to her hotel. We sat down at a table in the airport to discuss a price. I agreed to pay approximately 4300RMB which today in 2022 is around $664USD for three nights. She called a hotel shuttle to come and pick me up.

A van with no markings pulled up with two Chinese men in it. It was close to 8:00 p.m. now, and I get into the van. I was hungry, thirsty, and exhausted. Unintentionally I'd been fasting. *"This was very important to start my healing process."* As they shuttled me to the hotel, I was looking out the window while we were driving. There were no gas stations, no shops, no city, nothing. We seemed to be driving on an open road leading into a forest. About forty-five minutes later, the driver, made a left turn into one of the biggest cities I've ever seen in my life. There were skyscrapers everywhere, and all of the buildings were blacked out with no electricity. There were a couple of street lights on the road we were driving on, but that was it. I thought to myself, "What is this place? Where am I?"

I honestly never felt afraid, but I was in a weird daze from traveling over a day and some hours with hardly any sleep, food, or water. This was the first time in my life, I had gone so many hours without a solid meal. I wished I'd eaten more on the flight to Hong Kong. We were now driving down a dirt road through this city for another ten minutes when I saw a big lighted arrow pointing left. I thought to myself, *"This has got to be the hotel."* Sure enough, it was the hotel. The lobby lights were on, but I didn't see any of the room lights on from outside the building. "What Have I gotten myself into? What is this?" When we pulled up to the hotel, there were four Chinese men standing on the steps nicely dressed in three-piece suits. They grabbed my luggage and escorted me to the hotel's reception counter.

I checked into the hotel, and something just didn't seem right. My phone service switched over from Verizon to China Air and I was able to use my phone. I asked the guy at the counter through Google Translate, "Where are all of the people?"

He responded on his translation device, "They're at dinner."

I again responded through Google Translate, "That's great," I replied. "I'm hungry. Where can I get some food and water? Where's the restaurant?"

He pointed to some snacks hanging on a wall. They didn't look very fresh. I declined buying any, and proceeded to the elevator to go up to my room.

I took the elevator up to the 11th floor. When the elevator door opened up, I stuck my head out to see if I could hear anyone talking. I looked left, and then right to see if anyone was on the floor. I didn't see or hear anyone. There was a stale smell that hit me as if the hotel was built years ago, but had never been occupied. As I was walking to my room, I looked up and noticed big black cameras pointing toward every door on the floor. I walked quickly to my suite, and when I got into my room, I immediately went to the window and opened the curtains so I could look out the window. I was looking for some land marks, and the airport. I couldn't see anything, only buildings. From here, I went to the restroom. As I was standing there using the restroom, there was a sign above the toilet that said, *"Forbidden, No Pornography, No Google, No YouTube, No Facebook, No Instagram, No Twitter."*

That's when I decided I wasn't staying at this hotel. I washed my face and brushed my teeth then grabbed my luggage and went down the elevator to the lobby. As I was leaving the hotel, the staff urged me to stay. Ignoring them, I walked to the dirt road we came from, and started down the road. As I'm walking down the dirt road, I saw an old man standing under a streetlight looking up at the sky.

I ran up to him and asked if he could get me a taxi back to the airport. He just stared at me. He didn't speak English. Though this was frustrating, I suddenly felt compassion for people in America who didn't speak English. The Universe was showing me a different perspective on life. I was seeing the world from a different lens. As I'm having this revelation, a taxi pulled up out of nowhere, and tried to wave me into the taxi. I tried to ask him if he was going to take me to the airport, but the taxi driver just looked at me like the old man under the street light did. I didn't get into the taxi. The last time I'd jumped into a van I ended up in a ghost city. I didn't have a clue where I was, so I decided to walk back to the hotel where I at least had cell phone service.

As I got back to the hotel, I decided to call my contact John from Winsun 3D. When I got ahold of John, he sounded panicked. He asked where I was since I didn't check in with him when I got off the plane. John spoke with the guy at the counter on the phone and convinced him to refund half of my money and shuttle me back to the airport.

As I waited for the shuttle to pick me up, a Greyhound-style bus arrived at the hotel, a bunch of people got off the bus full of laughter. They seemed excited to see me. They walked over to me, and started taking pictures with me smiling with their thumbs up! They made me feel like a superstar celebrity. This was a fun experience.

When I finally got back to the airport my phone switched over to china air. I called my wife and asked her to book me a nice familiar American named hotel that was close to the airport. I didn't care what the cost was. I just wanted to get some sleep. She found a JW Marriott, and this hotel became my embassy for the next three days. Thankfully, It had everything I needed to live comfortably while in China.

By the time I checked in, it was approximately 12:00 a.m. and I was beyond exhausted. When I got to my room, there were 2 bottles of water sitting on the desk. I immediately drank them and prepared for bed.

The following day when I woke up, my stomach was bubbling. Oh no, I ran as fast as I could to the restroom, and I barely made it to the toilet. Boom, Mississippi mud came out of my body. It wasn't your typical diarrhea. It was so gross. I'd never experienced anything like this! I'd gone almost three days without food now. My body was clearly cleansing itself from 38-years of toxins that were built up from my lifestyle. I remember looking in the mirror and thinking, "It's been years since I've had a flat stomach."

After I showered and got dressed, I headed out to explore but was unprepared for the China heat. I'd been to Texas and Florida in the summertime, but this heat felt like something from another planet. I didn't need a sauna to detox myself here. All I had to do was go outside. Mother Nature took care of the rest. John later told me that Chinese people don't go outside in the daytime, and it made perfect sense why.

That night, I finally ate dinner. My body was ready to put some food in it. I had an Australian grass-feed steak with vegetables and a Pepsi. Yep, I found Pepsi in China. Another item that poisons our bodies, but I felt like I had to have it!

I took a bite of the steak, and wow, it was absolutely amazing. The only time I'd ever had a steak like this in the States was at a high-end steak house. And the vegetables had so much flavor. For the first time in ten years, I could actually taste the food. I think the pain pills blocked my taste receptors in my brain. I'm loving life again. Something about this land made me feel like a better person. I wasn't having any worrisome thoughts. The energy here was a lot different than in California. It felt more vibrant. The people seemed to pay attention to details and were very friendly to me!

Over the next three days, I didn't eat much solid food it was too hot. I did eat some noodle plates, fruit, and drank a lot of water. The fruit was also the best tasting fruit I had eaten in years. Everything I ate in China had great flavor. I give all of the food I ate an A+.

On my last day, I had my meeting with the 3D company. They showed me all their 3D printed products and I was amazed. *"Pinch me, I'm in the future."* I wished I could have spent more time there, but my visa was set to expire. I went straight to the airport from the R&D Center in Suzhou. Since my prior travel arrangements in the beginning of my trip were delayed, I didn't have a returning fight home. Thankfully, my wife found me one since it was last minute. As I was boarding the plane, one of the airline's employees pulled me from the line and told me that my seat had been upgraded to business class. This made me very happy since my trip was everything but smooth.

I happened to sit next to a pharmacist who lived in San Diego. He was on his computer working and I couldn't help but glance over at his screen. There was a picture of a dead lab rat with its belly opened up and I had to ask, *"What are you working on?"*

"I'm reviewing the results from a new vaccine that we developed." He said.

"What type of vaccine?" I asked.

"A vaccine to cure tumors." He said.

"Wait a minute. How did you know that specific rat had the tumor?" I asked.

He looked at me and said, *"How do you think?"*

I said, *"I don't know. Enlighten me."*

"We gave it the tumor. Then we came up with a vaccine to cure it." He said.

I asked, *"So, how do people get tumors?"*

He explained that they'd used tissue cells from the rat's foot to create the tumor. Then they'd inject the rat with the tumor cells. That's how he knew which rat had the tumor.

"If the pharmacist was able to give this particular lab rat a tumor, what do you think they can give us?" I thought. This conversation disturbed me. Are we all just (human) lab rats? There's a lot of money to be made with sick people. How many people are suffering from unnatural, curable diseases. This conversation made me dedicated to taking care of my physical body. I'm a powerful human on earth with the capabilities to heal myself.

When I arrived back to LAX, I noticed a different vibe as soon as I got off the plane. Everyone seemed to be moving so slowly. I must of acclimated to the energy of China. I didn't know what was happening to me, and nothing seemed real in my life anymore, something was off. I could feel it. The life I've come to know over the last 15-years was starting to change.

Second Trip

I was invited back to China by the 3D printing company for a press conference they hold each year in late August of 2018. This time, I planned out my stay and knew how to catch the Maglev train—a bullet train powered by magnet—to Shanghai from PVG airport. China's architecture is beyond amazing. This country is light-years ahead of the U.S. in technology.

On my flight to China, I was wishing I had some cannabis with me. I was going to be in China for ten days this time (I wanted to adjust to the time difference before the press conference), and knew I'd have a craving for it. It was my go-to medicine for everything now.

I arrived in China 4-days early, and I wasn't feeling very energetic this time around. I found myself sleeping more than usual. I was craving some cannabis and I was wishing I had some.

The morning of the press conference, I woke up feeling a little nervous. I had a light breakfast and went to the hotel pool for a swim to calm myself. I just wanted to smoke a joint. This was when I knew it was time for me to get serious about quitting cannabis. I was trying to start a new life for me and my family, but now I was thinking more about smoking cannabis instead of my goals. This was not good in my opinion. I like the ideas I had when I used cannabis. The problem was that I'd get so many great ideas but I wouldn't be sober long enough to go after them. I was creating too many realities in my mind.

The universe must have picked up what I was putting out. When I arrived at the press conference, I was escorted to my seat, which was next to some builders from Kenya. We introduced ourselves, and had a brief conversation about construction. As we were talking, three other guests arrived. One of them seemed to be drunk. He was loud and acted as if he knew me. He sat down next to me and says, "I can't believe you made it."

I had no idea who this guy was. I looked at him a little confused and said, "Yup, I'm here." He then pulls out a pen that resembles a wax pen for cannabis, and holds it next to me. Without thinking, I grabbed it, and took a hit. It was empty, but after I took a hit, I shook my head and asked him, "What was that?"

He said, "Its my wax pen. I don't go anywhere without it."

The universe never seems to amaze me anymore. I had cannabis on my mind that entire day. When I got to the place I was supposed to be, God delivered my request. Even though the pen was empty, it took the craving off my mind, but I wasn't happy with myself. I was in a foreign country and I didn't know who this guy was. Who knows what could have been in that pen? If I was going to do international business, I needed to make a lot better decisions. This was a learning experience for me.

When I got back to my hotel, I took a long, hard look at myself in the mirror. I said to myself, "I'm six thousand miles away from where I come from, and I'm still attracting the same experiences in my life.

This trip had been an eye-opener for how much more I needed to grow. Looking back, I never should have taken a hit from his pen. It could have been poison. I need to be more careful while traveling abroad. In hindsight, I must have been vibrating to that frequency, and attracted him into my world. In actuality, I'm starting to notice how powerful my mind is when I truly want something. The universe seems to always deliver no matter what it is.

On my flight home, I once again sat in business class, this time next to two guys. One guy had no arms. He was in China getting fitted for some new prosthetic robotic arms that would be connected to a chip in is brain. He would then be able to move his arms and fingers like a person normally would. I thought this would be cool to put in the book to give hope for people with no limbs. Science is working on something great for you in the near future. The other guy said he was a hacker from Malaysia. I didn't get into a deep conversation with him about that. I thought he was trying to hack me for some reason.

Back in California, I felt more vibrant than ever, but the people there didn't appear to be on my level of feeling. The people in a low state of vibration seemed to be walking around as empty vessels with no soul. They almost looked like projected holograms to me. This kind of freaked me out.

That night I ate a steak with mashed potatoes filled with butter and a glass of cow milk which made me bloated. This was the last time I ever drank cow milk. My trip to China has really opened my eyes and made me think deeply about the food we eat. I'm starting to believe there's an underline reason to why our food isn't GMO free. I think it has a lot to do with vibration. Is this done deliberately, or is it by accident?

I explained my trip to China for the simple fact that I was basically on my final leg of recovery. At home, I had a terrible diet, I was over-weight, and I still got urges to take pills sometimes. I know without a shadow of a doubt in my heart that the universe arranged this entire trip to help me detoxify my body and teach me how to take care of it with proper foods. I was also being shown a different perspective on life traveling in a foreign country and not able to communicate like I did in the States. Finally, I was being shown how cannabis was affecting my life negatively in my business, or was the cannabis separating me from my business so I could finish healing myself to become a healer? Only time will tell, but wile on the pills I lived in an egotistical world, and on cannabis, I lived in a more peaceful relaxed world more connected with nature. At the time, I felt like I was living in between two separate worlds.

Scotland QLA Seminar

Around the same time I came across the 3D printed castle on LinkedIn, I watched an episode of the "Joe Rogan Experience podcast." His guest was Dan Pena who was dressed in a three-piece suit and talked like a sailor just like my dad. In fact, he reminded me a lot of my dad in how he carried himself. In the episode, Dan talked a lot about money and how someone could become a millionaire starting from scratch buying businesses. I watched the entire interview as much of what he said about life resonated with me. Afterwards, I started evaluating the people around me and the direction I was headed. I knew I wanted to go to his castle seminar in Scotland. I wanted to do something different. I was tired of the contracting business. Looking back, I know the Universe made this happen. I always seem to get what I asked for.

I applied and was accepted to Dan Pena's Quantum Leap Advantage seminar. In October 2018, just before I left for Scotland, I received a phone call from the 3D printing company inviting me for one last business trip to China, days before the seminar. In hindsight, I think the Universe was trying to protect me from losing my focus on 3D printing. My ego didn't want to listen. I flew to Edinburgh, Scotland from Shanghai in October 2018.

For nine days, I stayed at Guthrie Castle and was waited on by butlers while I learned how to build a board if directors to buy and sell business for my future business endeavors. I was focused on becoming more successful and dedicated to my task. We would have class in the morning starting at 8:00 a.m. till 6:00 p.m. dinner was at 7:00 p.m. After dinner, we would meet in the sitting room to go over our homework assignments that would be due in the morning before class started. I would be lucky to get to bed before 1:00 a.m. each day.

And the food? To say Dan Pena's chef was first class would be an understatement. I ate like an absolute king compared to when I was in China. We ate breakfast, lunch, and dinner with healthy snacks in between classes. I lost another thirteen pounds in fourteen days of traveling. I could never lose weight in the States, and now it was just falling off.

The highlights of this experience were learning how to set up a board of directors for a business acquisition team, boxing an opponent in the ring for two minutes, getting waited on by butlers, and eating the food. I didn't want to leave this lifestyle. It was definitely a few steps up from my old life, but it gave me a lot of motivation to become ultra-wealthy and create generational wealth for my family. After reflecting on this experience, Dan Pena was programming us to be ultra-rich and was instilling wealth into our minds through the environment we were living in. We need more of this type of living in the world.

In a taxi heading back to the airport in Edinburgh, I gazed out the window and noticed farm animals all over the hillsides. Everything was green and full of life. I'd learned during the seminar that the Scottish government opposed GMOs, and the difference in taste was obvious.

What the hell is going on with the food in the U.S.? Now that I was paying more attention to my body, I was realizing that there was definitely more to this issue than meets the eye. The air was crisp, and the people were nice in Scotland. As my vibration raised, I could feel how different the energy was in each country. China's energy felt busy, and upbeat with pockets of calmness. Scotland's energy felt calm, peaceful, and freeing. California's vibration felt like a mixed bag depression, hate, and worry with sporadic happy positive energy.

"We're all kings and queens. We're not supposed to be fat and walk around with diseases." From my experiences, I knew I needed to change how I ate while living in America. The food effects how I feel so I decided to go vegan for a year and a half to see how my body reacted. This decision ended up being life changing. I was able to consistently walk around at 165 pounds, and I became a more peaceful, loving person.

I was starting to connect the dots regarding what food was good for me and what wasn't, and the more I learned about good food and its health benefits, the more intrigued I became since I was starting to see results in the most positive ways. I was starting to have more energy, and my appearance was becoming younger looking. Good health was starting to become my new found passion.

I felt as if I'd been taken to school in the universal kingdom to see my future, yet I couldn't seem to move on to my "new" life I created. I would soon need to find myself.

CHAPTER FOUR
Finding Myself

"Man plans and God laughs. This phrase couldn't have rung truer for me. I wasn't in a good place mentally after I returned from Scotland. I felt like a soldier coming back from overseas and everything was different. I'd been away from my family and business for close to three months in total. My kids were growing up so fast and I hardly recognized them. I could hardly recognize my wife. I felt as if my mind had been erased and re programmed to a new life. The only problem is, I was focusing on too many things at once. I had split energy and I almost programmed myself into a life I didn't want to live through the Bible."

My wife did her best to manage the business, but there was too much drama within the company over those years and I was ready for a change. I tried my hardest to keep my drywall company alive, but I lost control and my heart wasn't in it anymore. I couldn't find the "flow" that I once had.

I've been in so many different realities over the last three months, I just couldn't focus on one thing. I'd built up thirteen years of infrastructure, and when I returned from Scotland, my phone literally stopped ringing. My business was fading away to make room for what I was focusing on.

My ego was fighting my heart. I was torn between money and life. My ship was sinking, and I was faced with the question, *"How do I save a sinking ship?*

The answer was clear. *"let the ship sink."* I remember getting on the phone with my clients and employees telling them that I was done with the business. I didn't have the passion for it anymore. I was burnt out!

And so, in November 2018, I stopped working.

Looking back, I probably could have saved my business, as well as my marriage, but at what cost? I'd work so much that my wife and kids never got to be with me while I had a present state of mind. They never got to see the best side of me. The pills with the business almost killed me and stole the best years of my family's life with me.

But once I was at home every day, I felt as if I didn't even know who my wife and kids were. I didn't know who

I was anymore. I didn't know how to comfort them, or be a real husband or father. I used to get pissed off at myself thinking about how I let these pills take over my life—the life I'd sworn would never happen as a kid. In hindsight, I'm grateful the Universe kept me at work while I was addicted to the pills. My energy at the time would have been toxic to my kids.

I was so wrapped up in my business goals, I had an everything's my way or the highway mentality. Then once I lost my business, tension mounted as I couldn't take care of my family monetarily any longer. I wasn't the same person energetically or vibrationally. I was still balancing out my body from the years of opioid abuse. I didn't know what was real or fake anymore. My wife would encourage me to get back to work, but I would resist.

For some reason, I started reading the Bible my uncle gave me while I was traveling back and forth to China. I was starting to feel lost with no direction, so I dove deep into it. I read the Bible five or six times while smoking weed opening up my spiritual gate to soak this book into my mind. Everything seemed crystal clear to me. But instead of making me feel better, the Bible made me feel worse. I took everything I was reading to be literal.

I decided to find a church in which I felt comfortable, and soon I found one in Southern California. On my first visit, they welcomed me and made me feel at home. Then they told me that if I wanted to understand the Bible better, I needed to go to the Bible school they held on Wednesday nights.

When I arrived that first Wednesday, after smoking some cannabis, I wasn't used to this type of environment. I didn't know why at the time, but the energy in the building made me feel sad.

They asked me if I wanted to sign up as a volunteer to be a servant of God. Since my transformation from being an egotistical human to a more loving one, I did so happily, liking the idea of signing up to help people. In late November 2018, there was a huge fire in Northern California called "The Camp Fire," and I wanted to help in some way, as I had some experience with this kind of disaster.

In 2003, there was a huge fire in San Bernardino. "The Old Fire," as it was known, threatened San Bernardino and Highland, as well as the mountain resort communities. Upwards of eighty-thousand people were evacuated. When the fire came down the mountain and started burning houses in the Del Rosa area, my friends and I quickly loaded furniture into our cars at my friend's house. I lived further away from the mountains, so I wasn't too worried about my house. Then we went next door and turned on his neighbor's automatic sprinklers. Next, we used water hoses to soak the roofs of the nearby houses that didn't have automatic sprinklers. We figured if we could protect the neighbors' houses from burning, we would protect my friend's house. Thankfully, the plan worked.

Despite the intense fire and thick smoke, we refused to abandon his house, even when the fire department and sheriff came to evacuate us. After not complying with the order to leave, they hooked us up a fire hose to a fire hydrant, told us we were on our own, and left the scene. Unfortunately, the fire hose wasn't connected to a fire truck to pressurize the line, but we made use of the extra water.

Moments later, one of the houses behind my friend's caught fire, and my friend's brother jumped on the roof with a water hose. But when he got to the middle of the roof, he fell through into the house. In that moment my heart sank into my stomach. We all screamed and yelled his name. Moments later, he emerged unscathed. This was when we started to take the fire seriously. We all gathered around my friend's house and used our water hoses to keep everything wet. We saved four houses from burning that day.

Looking back, we had a day filled with adventure. I know were lucky that nobody got seriously hurt. We mostly had difficulty breathing and sore eyes from the smoke for a few days afterwards.

And so, when I got an email from the Southern California church asking for help assisting the victims of the fire in Paradise, I immediately agreed, much to my wife's displeasure. I wish I'd listened to her. *(Men, do yourselves a favor and listen to your wives.)*

Despite her protest to me leaving, my wife dropped me off at the church, and I jumped into a van with five other men volunteering their time. When we got to Chico, we turned onto a road that leads into a mountain and pulled up to a gate, where the driver punched in a code.

"Where are we are going?" I asked the driver.

"To the hotel."

"I thought we were camping?"

"We had a change of plans," he said, driving through the gate as it unlocked. Then he drove down a road leading into a canyon."

"How far do we need to drive?" I asked, noticing I no longer had cell phone service.

"It's five-miles into the canyon," He said.

Sure enough, the canyon opened up, and there was a hotel. As I exited the van, I felt nervous energy pumping through my body. When I exited the van in China, I felt calm and relaxed.

As I un-loaded my stuff from the van, I noticed three crosses on top of the mountain. I don't know why, but I thought to myself, "I need to go up there to pray." As I took my stuff up to our room, I used the restroom and I noticed a pack of matches on top of the toilet bowl. I didn't think anything of it at that time. I just noticed it.

Then I went downstairs to meet the guys for orientation. We were told to approach the homeowners with sensitivity and to be careful walking around the burn sites.

After orientation, we all stood in line to get served dinner. I'd been fasting and watching my diet for the last three months, and now I was about to eat donated cafeteria food. I thought to myself, Jesus spoke about keeping our temples pure. Eating heavy food wasn't good for my temple. It lowered my energy and hurt my stomach. I ate it anyways, not having a healthier choice.

But as I ate, I started to receive negative thoughts run through my head. I kept feeling as if I wanted to cry. Maybe I was picking up on other people's vibrational energy? The volunteers there were crying a lot.

After dinner, I decided to walk up the mountain in the dark to take a couple of hits of the joint I'd brought. When I reached the top of the mountain, I just start screaming at the top of my lungs: "I want to go home!" I didn't want to stay at the hotel with all of these people.

I sparked my joint to calm my nerves. That joint needed to last me a week I was thinking. When I was done taking a hit from my joint, I sat there pondering how I got into this situation. When I started walking back down the mountain, I suddenly got an urge to stop walking and grabbed my flashlight. I was standing at the edge of a cliff. I took this as a sign from the universe that my life was heading in the wrong direction. I shouldn't have gone on this trip.

When I got back to our room, nobody was in there. They were all downstairs doing a Bible study by the fire. When I opened up my suitcase, the matchbook that was on the toilet when I first got there was inside my suitcase. *What the hell?* Is someone trying to send me a message that they were watching me, or is someone messing with me? But why? That night was a horrible one. I ended up staying up all night watching my back. I didn't trust these fools, and to make matters worse, I was farting all night while listening to five other men fart from the dinner we ate. The room had a foul smell and nobody could control it.

In the morning, we got up at 6:00 a.m. to read a daily devotional from the Bible and eat breakfast before we were assigned to our disaster teams. Upon arrival to our first burn site. I was assigned to work with the team leader sifting buckets of ash materials. We basically would put ash onto a screen, and then shake it looking for valuables.

The team leader told me that I needed to learn how to find coins. She then started hiding coins in the materials to teach me to how to find them. "We found a truckload of gold and silver bars at one house," she told me. They were taken to an undisclosed location." I just nodded. I had no idea why she was telling me this. It seemed very odd. After about an hour of sifting materials, she assigned me to dig in locations marked with flags—places where the homeowners thought their valuables might be found. I didn't like going through people's stuff looking for jewelry, coins, or gold bars. I thought we were going to help remove debris and clean everything up. We were basically treasure hunters. But I did as I was asked and ended up finding a small bucket full of old collectible coins. I gathered them and immediately gave them to the homeowner, who was amazed I'd found them.

He said he didn't care about the coins, so I just stood there and talked to him about my experience in

San Bernardino, and how our city overcome the various challenges of rebuilding. The conversation gave him hope. He told me I made him feel better talking with him. It felt good to help lift his spirits. Before we left this burn site, all of the volunteers held hands to form a prayer circle, and the team leader said a prayer. As we held hands, I started to get an overwhelming vibration of sadness come over me. Looking back, I can see that we were transferring energy through each other. This was why I started to have negative feelings flow through me. I was getting a dose of everyone's feelings collectively while holding hands.

When we got back to the hotel, I didn't feel very good. I wasn't energetic or happy and I felt like my energy was drained. Once again, I hiked up to the crosses on the mountaintop to take a couple hits of my joint. Ahhhhhh, I feel better. I sat on top of the mountain by myself just looking at all of the hills in nature, enjoying my own company and reflecting on all of my adventures I'd been through the last few months. *How did I wind up here?* I was starting to think that my life was a movie, and I was the producer. I need to change the scene quick!

I head back down the mountain to go eat dinner. When I got back inside the hotel, I happened to get into a conversation with one of the Chaplins. I stated my displeasure with my day. The Chaplin said, "What did you think you came here for?"

I told him, "To help people. Not to dig for gold and coins. There were a lot of families with no place to go, and we're digging for treasure." My comments didn't sit well with him.

After dinner, everyone moved to the reception hall, where there was a huge fire pit. Most of the people were reading Bibles. Some were playing music, and others were having friendly chats. Then there were two guys sitting on a couch with computers open, deep in conversation. The two guys on the couch weren't like the other people. I could tell they were more about business. I overheard them discussing future business on how to get more donations so they could buy a building somewhere in Chico. This didn't sit well with me for some reason. Maybe it was the weed, or maybe the weed gave me enough courage to stand up and ask them, "Why aren't you using the donation money to build temporary shelters? Every person here paid to be here and help, yet all we're doing is digging for treasure and praying in hand holding circles. I could do a lot more with my talent." This ruffled their feathers. I didn't know if the cannabis was helping me or getting me into trouble. I felt as if I'd said exactly what I was supposed to say at that very moment.

The next morning after breakfast, when I was walking to the van, one of the guys who'd been sitting on the couch the night before came up to me and pulled me aside. "I admire your passion for wanting to help people," he said, while looking me in the eye. "You're different. Man doesn't understand you, but God does." He then walked away. I didn't know how to feel after that comment.

At the burn site I'd been assigned to for the day, the team leader walked up to me and pulled out a fake rat from her overalls and said, "Did you put this in my lunch?"

I looked at her while shaking my head and said, "I wouldn't do something like that. What are you trying to tell me?"

"Make sure you don't talk to the homeowners," she said. "You're only here to help dig. We don't want to give the homeowners the wrong impression."

I had no idea what she was talking about. The homeowner I'd spoken with had been thankful for the conversation. This was I started watching my back. I needed to find a way out of this mess. I didn't bring any money with me, and I didn't have my truck. As we closed out the day, all I could think about was going home.

At the end of day three, yet another day of digging and sifting, I headed up the mountain before dinner to smoke my joint. While there, the thought of working out crosses my mind. The thought sounded good, so I decided to head down to the gym on the property. As I approached the gym, I could hear rap music playing Tupac's song, "All Eyes on Me" and I started nodding my head to the beat. When I tried to open the door, it was locked. I heard people inside the gym. It sounded as if they were having a party.

I knocked on the door, and a teenage boy opened it. He was working out with a couple of friends. This trip was getting weirder and weirder. "What are you guys doing?"

I asked. They just said "Nothing." Noticing a pool table, I asked if they wanted to play. They declined and kept working out.

"Is this a Christian disciple school?" I thought. It doesn't seem like a holy place.

As I'm thinking this, a guy that drove up to Paradise with us walked in. Seeing the teenagers, he shook his head and asked them to turn off the music. They ignored him. I thought it was pretty funny, but he didn't. I could see him get angry, so I pulled him back and suggested he just play pool with me. By this point, I was truly over this trip. "I want to kick their asses," the guy kept saying.

"If you put your hands on them, you'll have to deal with me," I said. Maybe this is was why I'd been led down there? To see what this organization was about, and to protect the kids.

Later that night, we all gathered around the fire in the reception area again. I was talking to a random guy about our vices. While I was telling a story, one of the guys on our team, named Mark, walked over, pulled out a huge Bowie Knife, and set it on the table in front of the chair I was sitting on next to a cell phone with the microphone pointed toward me. He then went and stood by the wall, where he stared at me while trying to intimidate me. I knew this church group was trying to scare me into keeping my mouth shut about all of my adventures and manifestations, and I wasn't intimidated, but I did stop talking.

After I'd been silent for about fifteen minutes, Mark walked over to retrieve the knife and cell phone.

"That wasn't very Christian of you, Mark," I said, as he walked away. He looked at me but didn't say anything. I started to wonder whether I'd seen something that they wanted to keep secret, or if they were just tired of me talking with people. They'd put the matches in my suitcase the first day we arrived. I'd known something wasn't right from the start. In hindsight, I was the only volunteer talking about my pill addiction, traveling to other countries, and business. When there wasn't any haters around, I was telling stories to keep people entertained. I was a free spirit sharing experiences. I probably should have just kept my face in the Bible like most of the others, but I was tired of reading it. I felt like it was programming my mind to think and feel a certain way.

On day five, though, I had a sense that I was about to be sent home. I was calm and relaxed. On our way to the first burn site, there was a tree lying in the road. A crew was chopping it up. We soon learned this project had gotten canceled. *YES!* I thought.

We headed to the second project site only to hit a detour and then another detour. When we finally pulled up to the house, the homeowners weren't there. They'd canceled. *YES!* The Universe was working in my favor today.

The project at the third burn site we pulled up to was delayed due to the owners' not being present. When the homeowners arrived, the Universe called in the form of my wife. I walked away from the group so I could talk with her as the group gathered in a circle to pray as they always did. Once they were done praying, the team leader came over and said I was done. They were sending me home for not participating in their prayer. I was jumping for joy! I'd just known today was going to be a great day.

They drove me to Chico and put me on a bus home. My joy quickly dissipated. Now I had to deal with reality, which was that I wasted my time going up north. I honestly thought that I would have been able to provide 3D printed shelters to the displaced fire victims. I should have stayed home to take care of my family.

Gaining Clarity

I respected Jesus's teachings, but I didn't like the church mentality. I felt like a slave for a cult generating profit from a natural disaster digging for valuables. I was confused about how to please God, and in my own confusion, I forgot how to please myself which is an expression of God. I was caught in a mental trap that ended up costing me everything I loved in this world—my wife, and kids. I'd looked to the Bible for direction, but I became more lost. Even Christians thought I'd lost touch with reality. I was overly obsessed with reading the Bible and witnessing on the streets trying to convert people to Christianity. Yup, I was that crazy guy trying to save people while they walked their dogs at the dog park. In hindsight, I'm having a good laugh as I write this. *We live and we learn!*

I started to give the church the little money we had left because in the Bible I'd read passages like this and took them literally.

For Example: Luke 21:1-4, Jesus looked up and saw the rich putting their gifts into the offering box, and he saw a poor widow put in two small copper coins, and he said, "Truly, I tell you, this poor widow has put in more than all of them. For they all contributed out of their abundance, but she out of her poverty put in all she had to live on." My interpretations caused my family even more financial hardship.

How could I have gotten things so wrong? At church, the pastor on the pulpit would preach about how all the lost souls looking for answers, just had to pray, and then seal their prayers with a tithe to the church.

"You want me to pray? WTF are you talking about? Please guide me more", I was losing everything.

Why was this happening to me? Why did I pick up this book? Why did I read it while smoking weed? At the time it made so much sense. I started floating from church to church, looking for help and answers. To make a long story short, I decided to just focus on myself outside of the church.

1 John 3:17 says, "But whoever has the world's goods, and sees his brother in need and closes his heart against him, how does the love of God abide in him."

After over a year of trying to fit into the mold of the church, I concluded that I had to learn how to take care of myself again. I needed to put in the work to finish healing and re-programming myself that started in China. It was time to stop going to church and listen to my inner guidance. Religion just wasn't working for me.

I'd never followed the crowd. I'd always followed myself. Looking to others for help only made me feel more lost. God couldn't help me if I didn't help myself. I had to put in the work to get healthy, and start thinking for myself again. The first step to healing was through fasting.

This wasn't to say the Bible and the church hadn't helped me, because it did. I'd used Jesus's teachings to heal my physical body and calm my mind. And then I'd used my gut instincts to take myself out of an unhealthy situation. I had to step out of the box of religion, because I was not built to follow someone else's path, I'm built lead my own path!

When "eye" woke up, I realized that I'd shifted my reality to that of religion by putting my attention and energy to it. I'd been unknowingly creating multiple realities for months now.

I'd gone to China to learn about technology but had ended up learning more about nutrition and how to purify my body for healing. This was the real prize.

I'd gone to Scotland to learn how to buy and sell businesses. The program wasn't a fit for me at that time, but Dan Pena had shown me a world of abundance and healthy food. This was the real prize.

And I'd gone to Paradise, Ca to be of service to others. Instead I'd learned that I needed to continue working on myself. This was the real prize.

Looking back, I was grateful for this opportunity to examine myself. Maybe the weed was hindering my thought processes and decision-making? Or was it opening my spiritual eye, so I could see. Only time will tell.

CHAPTER FIVE
Committing to Health

"I thought I would jump back on the horse and thrive in my old life right off the bat. I thought when I got off the pills, my life was going to take off. When I got off the pills, they took me off of the vibrational frequency I was calibrated to the last 13-years of my life. When I started smoking cannabis, the plant put me on a different vibrational frequency. I was in between my inner and outer world. How do I bring my inner world into reality?

When I was on the pills, my world was outside of me and I was manifesting the pain I felt on the inside. When I was smoking cannabis, my world was inside of me and I was living in my greatness.

I didn't know which one was real. As it turned out, the world outside of myself was a reflection to how I felt on the inside. My clock was about to expire. Hence, all of my accidents in Chapter Two. I was living in another vibrational world on the doctor prescribed drugs."

By the beginning of 2019, my wife and kids believed I lost my mind. Looking back, I can see that I did lose my mind. I felt like I went into the future, but came back to the past, and was unable to live in the present moment. When I was on pills, I never thought about the past or future. I was always in the present moment, creating my life. When I was smoking cannabis to get off the pills, I was always thinking about the future and was never truly in the present moment enjoying life.

Finally, it all came to a head. I don't blame my wife for leaving me. After losing our house from my lack of production, I moved into my office in Riverside, California, my wife moved into her sisters with the kids. My brother would come to visit and bring me food and money, but for the most part, I wanted to be by myself. I was completely breaking down my body and mind to continue purifying both.

While going through my purification process, I started to walk around the city during the day, and I'd notice all the homeless people. I hadn't paid attention to them in the past, when I was running my company. At the time, I didn't realize that I was living in a different dimension of reality. I felt as if—the Universe was showing me myself since I had become homeless and the other homeless people were a reflection of my situation. I hated it, so I tried to help them even though I needed help.

I had a bunch of left-over building materials from when I was contracting, so my brother and I started to make little shelters with wheels that they could roll around the city, but whenever I'd check up on people we'd given the shelters to, I'd find them slamming heroin in them. This would piss me off. The Universe was showing me that unless the homeless people in California wanted to change, they weren't going to change, and I was wasting my time giving them a place to chill and do drugs. (Of course, this wasn't the case with every person I met on the streets. Some didn't do drugs but simply preferred to live for free on the streets and were perfectly happy.)

Even though curing the homeless issue's an important task to complete, my thoughts started to shift. *Our kids are the real future,* I realized. *We need them to fulfill their potential.* I didn't want them to think it was normal to see people living on the streets doing drugs. This wasn't good programming for their minds. How could the perception of the homeless population be changed?

I came to a couple of conclusions:

- We needed to get these people off the streets so we can raise the vibration of the area. Their thoughts with negative vibrations stick to people, and they are attracting low-vibrational energy in the form of more homeless people to the city like a magnet.
- Or I just needed to move my family's energy to a location with no poverty, crime, or bad vibes.

The time on my own opened my eyes to the truth of this world. For instance, if you go into a city and see a lot of poverty, crime, drugs and homelessness. This is an indication that the city is starting to die. *Manifestation is real,* I thought. *We manifest what we feel inside.* Many of the homeless people I met were collectively manifesting the world they were living inside of themselves into their outer reality for all to see. They weren't thinking with their right minds. And I should know—I was right there with them. I just needed to observe and learn.

Printing sustainable communities using 3D technology would solve housing problem, but how do you fix the person's inner world if they don't want to change? I had to surrender to the idea that maybe the problem wasn't mine to fix right now. Maybe all I could do was fix the world inside myself.

Back on the Road

In June 2019, I received I an email from the Winsun 3D. They were inviting me back to China for another press conference. I jumped at the chance. I've been living in my office with no bed or shower for months. Now, I could go back to the place where I'd begun my transformation.

My brother and I picked up a small project to generate some money for the trip, and in July, I made my way back to China. I started to fast the day I left America. I used the invitation back to China as a reason to fast and purify my body. "In the Bible. Jesus was always talking about fasting and purification of the temple which is your body, and the mind to bring forth the energy (spirit) inside of you."

I fasted for almost three days and I spent most of my time sleeping in my nice comfortable bed at the hotel. I started noticing my appearance changing. I lost more weight, which was a good thing at this time, and my skin looked younger and more vibrant. Maybe I was tapping into something? I was still in the process of learning about my body and its capabilities. There was something about the energy in the form of people on this land that just made me feel amazing. I felt at peace.

Once I returned to the U.S., I felt as if I had to keep traveling. Every time I returned from China, I felt as if I brought their positive energy back with me. I wanted to keep exploring the earth. I felt like I needed to learn more about what was good for my body and what wasn't.

Luckily, the Universe took me on a few adventures to find out.

One day in 2019, I received a thought to travel the United States. I took a train to Chicago and went to church. The pastor at this church in Chicago I was listening to on YouTube claimed to have healing powers and preached about wanting to help the inner city in various ways, so I wanted to talk with him about my ideas regarding building 3D printed, eco-friendly, self-sustaining communities off the grid to help lower the cost of living for families, so parents could spend more time with their kids. I'd also been considering the idea of building wellness centers for people to heal from living life. Unfortunately, I wasn't able to get a meeting with him. Maybe I should have called first.

The same day I visited church, I took a taxi back to the train station to head back to California. Turns out the ticket price went up and I didn't have enough money to take the train back to California but the price was cheaper on Tuesday, so I ended up staying on the streets of Chicago for two nights. I wasn't scared. The shows I'd seen on TV made Chicago sound like a war zone at the time, but I didn't notice anything like this. I met several people that were homeless and explained my plans to build 3D Printed communities. They loved my ideas. One person told me, "When your back is up against the wall you'll find a way," but as the months went by, though, I begun to feel this wasn't my path.

Chicago reminded me of Los Angeles though the downtown was nicer and cleaner. Chicago's homelessness problem wasn't like California's. The people I met didn't seem to be on drugs and seemed tougher and more resilient due to the harsh weather they endure. It was cold at night, though I wasn't prepared for that type of weather. I didn't sleep very well. My heart goes out to those still living on the streets. Their living a hard energy draining life and have lost hope for the most part.

Shortly after I returned to California, I happened to receive a call from an old client for drywall work. I used the money I earned to rent a car. I had no purpose in mind but felt compelled to have another adventure. My first stop was Las Vegas. Here, I started to incorporate meditation into my fasting practice that carried over from China. I learned some techniques through various videos on YouTube. While meditating in my hotel room one day, waiting for my spirit to lead me to my next destination, I started to get thoughts of mountains and driving up north. Later that day, while walking on the Vegas strip, I started to see several signs with "Utah" on them. So, the next day, I drove to Salt Lake City.

When I was driving into Utah, I noticed several billboards with messages fighting against opioid abuse. I'd never seen billboards like this in California. I felt as if my purpose was crystallizing. I'd stopped using pain pills on my own, so maybe I could help others do so? I spent two days in in Utah, and during my stay, I continued fasting and taking it easy. I was completely cleansing my body again. I didn't know why, but I was. On my second day in town, I went for a drive, and noticed a shop promoting CBD to relieve anxiety and other ailments. I got a clear urge from my spirit to go into that shop.

While I was chatting with the owner, a woman withdrawing from opiates came in looking for help. The owner placed a few drops of CBD oil under her tongue and then sold her a bottle, which cost almost one hundred dollars.

After the woman left, I told the owner that I tested products on my body to see if they were safe, and I'd do a report on the side effects of this product. (CBD labels don't list any side effects). I mentioned that I'd been fasting for two days and had purified my body. "I have a clean pallet to work with." I said.

The owner said I was doing a good thing and that he was interested in my findings. He then gave me a dropper full under my tongue. I went back to the hotel and waited to see if I'd experience any side effects. Sure enough about forty minutes later, I got a headache along with a runny nose. As my heart started to beat faster than normal, my hands and feet started to sweat. I was hoping to feel relaxed. My body was rejecting the CBD product. I hadn't expected these results. The side effects went away after about an hour and a half. I did a report, and shared my findings with the owner who found my report interesting.

As my curiosity piqued, I decided to try CBD oil from another shop in Utah while my body was clean, but the shop worker here refused to let me sample the product and got aggressive with me. This sparked my interest even more. *Maybe this CBD thing is a bunch of smoke and mirrors,* I thought. Maybe it was sold to people who couldn't distinguish the benefits from the side effects.

I'd heard of CBD helping people who had seizures, but I believe these people get their CBD product from a known source that wouldn't compromise the hemp with chemicals, fillers, and additives. As I researched some CBD companies, the more I got the feeling that most CBD companies on the stock market were probably in the game for the money, not for health and wellness. Remember, CBD Oil is designed to go under your tongue and absorb into your blood stream. The blood then takes the CBD to every single cell of your body. This is not good if you're not getting a quality product. Choose your products wisely. Find a local source that grows and extracts the CBD Oil organically, or grow the hemp yourself!

I stayed in Utah for one more night. The next morning, I kept thinking about going to Austin. Unable to get the thought out of my head, so I booked a flight to Texas, and flew out that day. I arrived to find a city that was alive and vibrant—a complete 180 compared to Salt Lake City. Salt Lake City felt dead to me. I wondered if the opioid crisis in Utah was a much bigger problem than I'd imagined.

I did a Google search for CBD shops in Austin and headed to one downtown that sold hemp flower decarboxylated and made into an herbal tea. I hadn't eaten that day, and my body was as pure as it could be. When I drank the hemp tea. This time, I didn't have any noticeable adverse side effects. I felt relaxed and calm. I told the owner that she had a good tea. She wasn't promoting it to heal anything specific, it was just a medicinal shop.

The message was clear: I had to let my own body tell me what was good for me, and what wasn't. And I could only know this if my body wasn't full of crappy food and drinks so many of us consume every day. It was a reminder that each of us is the ultimate judge of our own bodies.

When I returned from my trip, I spent time reflecting on what I'd learned but had no idea what to do with the information. What I knew for sure was that I needed to get my shit together when it came to my health and finances. This has become my primary focus.

As I changed my diet, I found myself becoming a more loving person. During this time, I started my spiritual journey and started to write this book.

Although I already started a meditation practice, I stumbled across meditation (with)—breathing exercises on YouTube. I started learning how to do the breath of fire, pranayama, and Wim-Hof breathing method. The exercises made me feel good, so I dove deeper. Once I felt comfortable with these, I combined them to create a meditation practice that worked for me.

First, I'd do twenty minutes of breathing to help clear my mind of thoughts. Once I finished breathing, I'd sit quietly or with some soft music. As I did, I'd start to feel energy buzzing around the top of my head. Over time, I felt myself becoming more energetic, and my appearance continued to change. I was looking younger and more vibrant. I was able to feel the energy around me and see the world differently without the high of the cannabis.

For me, meditation became a tool that allowed me to see myself in other people. It allowed me to see the parts of myself that I needed to work on and change, and to see the parts of myself that I loved in other people. As I sit quietly, nothing even matters.

By 2020, I wasn't smoking cannabis as much anymore. I couldn't find any "clean" weed (without any chemicals in or on it)

After all the work I'd done purifying my body, I was able to taste the nutrients in the weed if it hadn't been flushed out properly. The flushing process takes approximately seven days of watering with RO/ or spring water only. The side effects I experienced from cannabis that hadn't flushed properly included headaches, cottonmouth, paranoia, or cravings for the chemical in or on the weed. I also had less energy and was less focused with the tainted spiritual medicine.

It was important for me to stay on my healing journey over the course of 2020, as it was one of the lowest vibrational years I'd ever witnessed in my forty years of existence on this planet. I continued eating healthy foods and focused on being creative (Hence, why I started writing this book).

For the first part of the year, I decided to make connections with the big players in the automated construction space for 3D concrete printing. I was still thinking of ways I could use this technology to make a positive impact on society. I started to learn more about how this equipment worked, as well as the different makes and models provided by several companies. I connected with seven of the largest companies via email, or phone calls to get manuals on the machines.

I also wrote an eighteen-page proposal with a four-page housing plan for how to 3D print eco-friendly self-sustaining housing off grid with a farm, which would be used to house and feed the homeless population. People could live here and take care of themselves until they were clean from any drugs and wanted to get back into society. I tried to connect with government officials, non-profits, and churches in California and Las Vegas, wanting to show them the proposal without success. I didn't receive even one phone call. After a few months of trying, feeling discouraged, I decided to set the project to the side for the future. The time wasn't right.

I decided to just keep focusing on my health and wellness. I was enjoying learning as much as I could about what foods were good and bad for my body through trial and error—well, it was mostly enjoyable; sometimes I'd get sick testing food on myself. It was astonishing to learn that most of the food on our grocery store shelves isn't good for the human body to consume. As a result, I now know why I was always tired and got bloody noses as a kid. I ate poorly.

And as I continued to heal the world inside of me, my outer reality became more peaceful and loving as well. My dedication to my healing journey showed me that everything and everyone in the Universe vibrates at a certain energy level.

I come to realize that we are all energy or spirits, in physical form vibrating at certain frequencies based on our lifestyles. The healthier we are, the higher the frequency we vibrate at giving us more energy. For example: When I felt like Shiite, I would attract experiences into my life that had the potential to start an argument or I would hit every red light. When I felt great and was vibrating high on the love boat, I would attract smiles, and green lights. It's like having two different families on earth at different ends of the vibrational spectrum. This is especially good to know if you're married. If one or both of you can hold a pure vibration in your relationship with no drugs or alcohol, you're probably living in heaven!

And I believe love is the highest vibration a human can hold. Even now, having shifted my internal vibration to one of peace and happiness, I'm still hoping to come together in a powerful manifesting relationship full of love in this lifetime. Two humans holding the vibration of love, happiness, peace, and prosperity can become very powerful creators. How do you know which vibration someone is on though? It's very simple, listen to how they speak. What are they talking about?

I thank the Universe every day for my new found health and awareness!

PART TWO

PERSONAL REVELATIONS

CHAPTER SIX

My Journey to Healing

"I went to public school in America. I was told to Pledge Allegiance to the flag. This was the start of my patriotism programming. I unknowingly became a soldier for this country right then. I was just a kid. Many others went on to enlist in the military, and risk their lives to fight overseas for this country's government.

But, there's another war going on for those that unknowingly enlisted through alcohol and drug use. The war's inside you. Divide and concur is the strategy.

At the time, I didn't realize that cleansing my mind and body from old thoughts and feelings were going to create a roller coaster of experiences in my life.

But looking back, *healing myself from within is how I won. When I purified my temple, I raised my energy and vibrationally re-connected to those on my vibration and my life started to change.*

We live in a liner spectrum of vibrational frequencies. I will do my best to explain how this works using the terms high and low frequency. Let's start with the basics.

ENERGY/VIBRATION/FREQUENCY:

1. Your source ENERGY or SPIRIT in a physical body.
2. You VIBRATE thoughts and emotions that attract or repel people and events.
3. These thoughts and emotions put you on a vibrational FREQUENCY attracting more of the same in the "form" of other people.

In essence, we're always connected to ourselves through other people. One way to understand what vibrational frequency you're on is to observe the people that come into your experience. I like to look at them as a mirror of myself.

Once you learn how to control your vibrational frequency, you can attract everything you need from the very spot you're at all day long. This is when you start to live in your own world CREATED BY YOU!!!!

The world projected through the news media, television shows, and radio is an external world most people are collectively attracted to. WHY? Because it's what they've been conditioned to pay attention too through years of cultural programming.

You're a very powerful creator on planet earth. YOU have very strong energy within the body. It's time we all learn how to consciously use this energy to create the lives of our dreams. If your life isn't going the way that you planned, I would recommend that you cleanse your energy body. I do this by shutting down my phone and going into nature for a few days to cleanse and reset myself from all of the thought creations I don't want to attract into my experience.

Some might ask, "since we're energetically vibrating our emotional state of being to everyone around us, how come I don't notice this?"

That's a very good question. The truth is, we all have been conditioned to react and feel a certain way for so long, and it's hard to know what our true feelings are anymore. We don't realize that our emotional state is being manipulated and we wonder why we're experiencing a roller coaster of emotions. We're in a vibrational war, and it's important to understand how your vibration matters. Below is an example to explain how we affect each other vibrationally.

Why do we pray for healing in church, and nine times out of ten nothing happens? The reason why nothing happens is because a lot of people in Church are not well themselves. The dominate vibration of un-wellness vibrates to and trough everyone. The dominate vibration will be the dominant frequency in the church. Have you ever walked inside a church and just wanted to cry? Have you ever walked inside a church and just wanted to dance? It's all about the dominate vibrational frequency. If more people raised their vibration with fasting, diet, exercise and meditation, the church would have a collective healing power to vibrationally heal people. In my experience meditating, I feel the energy buzzing through me and I do my best to radiate healthy vibrations.

I've traveled overseas and throughout the country over the last couple of years. I've been gathering useful information for this book. When I was cleansing, and purifying my body, my vibrational frequency was all over the place. I had to learn how to center myself. I always felt called to leave my surroundings because I couldn't cope with the differences in vibrational frequencies that people were radiating at the time. I didn't know what was happening to me.

The rulers of the outer world (Whomever it may be) need us in a low vibrational frequency. This frequency translates to fear, worry, hate, poverty, war and sickness to keep control over our emotional minds. We can collectively change this vibration by changing our personal vibration. In doing this, we will bring back our sovereignty one person at a time. We are vibrational creators of our reality. We are collectively vibrating together. If the world can get the collective consciousness into the vibrational reality that they portray on TV the dominate vibrational frequency, then that's the reality we will collectively vibrate too and live in. We are separated by vibration.

We are in a vibrational war, you can't see it, touch it, or taste it. This is why its called spiritual warfare. Thoughts send-off vibrations.

I have seen people protests on the news for justice. As humans we have compassion for brothers and sisters not treated fairly, but again, the rulers want to piss us off for the reaction. They create a problem, we react to the problem, and they give us the solution "they want!" This is why I don't watch TV anymore. I don't like the TV putting bad thoughts into my mind. I don't want to send out bad vibrational thoughts. Out of sight, out of mind.

Bible verse Philippians 4 verse 8 NIV: *Finally Brothers and sisters, whatever is true, whatever is noble, whatever is right, whatever is pure, whatever is lovely, whatever is admirable—if anything is excellent or praiseworthy—think about such things.*

I like creating my personal world. I'm more productive with my time now as a result. I live in my new vibrational reality free of hate, sickness, poverty, and war. I don't believe watching Bad TV programs like the news is healthy. I feel like the TV its being used as a weapon to program my mind into a reality I don't want to live in.

We need to protect our kid's minds. They are the most powerful vibrational creators. They are here to vibrationally create a new reality that's inside of them. Love, joy, happiness, compassion, and togetherness is the world they're sent here to create. Our kids come into this world programmed perfectly. We as parents let the world that corrupted us, corrupt them. As parents we have a huge responsibility to protect our kids from bad programming, but we only have a limited amount of time to have an influence over them. Ever wonder why kids are targeted to get hooked on drugs, or worse? It's because every child born is a vibrational solution to the current vibrational energy on earth.

When we're first born, we're the light of the world. I see how this world dimmed my light and put me in a low vibrational-frequency through doctor prescribed drugs and stress. I see from experience of being on both sides of the veil. Now that I regularly meditate and watch my diet, I can see and feel the difference in peoples' energy as I did when I was a kid. When I don't take good care of myself, I put myself into a vibration that picks up negative energy which translates into negative thoughts. I don't like that feeling. I like to keep my magnetic field strong. I do everything in my power to keep my energy high without man made supplements from a laboratory.

High frequency is the god frequency full of love, joy, happiness, compassion, and great ideas. Low frequency is the hell frequency I like to call it. This frequency is full of doubt, arguing, hate, anger, sickness, violence, and war.

If I'm in a high vibrational frequency, I will attract other high vibrational energy in people. If I'm in a low vibrational frequency, I will attract low vibrational energy in people. This is good to know in both business and in life. I want to attract the best version of myself

We all live in the universal kingdom, walking through the shadows of our life in the world. Maybe, I went through everything in my life to re-learn that the universal kingdom is pure divine love with no sickness, war, or poverty? As I continue to grow, I'm noticing almost everything is a mental state of mind. For example: Every city I go into has a specific state of mind. In order to tell if the city is healthy or not, I pay attention to the people, businesses, and overall wellness of a city. If I see a bunch of crime, poverty, and un wellness, then I view this part of the earth as having cancer that needs to be healed. The city has become a magnet for its overall energetic vibration.

The world I used to know through my phone, social media, TV, and radio (breed) war, hate, poverty, disease, homelessness, and crime to keep people in a low vibrational frequency. This is a false world projected on TV to program your mind into that reality. But why is this done? The only logical answer I can come up with is the people in control either know this information and it's the only way to keep people separated and divided for their control, or they know that their target audience loves to watch drama. The people in control of the media definitely know how to get people riled up.

The TV is a portal to your mind; you can turn it off and on. We all have a choice on what to watch and what not to watch. If you think the world is on fire, I want you to consciously try this; Walk outside, take a deep breath, and look around your surroundings. Smile and wave at someone because you're looking at the real world you live in through your own perception.

If you feel great, the world is great. If you feel like shit, you fall back into default programming of the world is on fire. I left the country and turned off the tv for a few months. This cleansed my mind. When I did this, I cleansed my mind from outside influences which opened up a new view of the world inside of me. If you can't change your surroundings, try to go into a neutral environment where there is less stimulation like nature. Nature is a great place to cleanse negative energy. Think of nature being the calm part of gods mind, and the big metropolitan city being the crazy, stressed-out sick part of gods mind that is spreading like wild fire throughout earth in this modern era. We need to stop this spread of cancer and take our power back.

I truly believe that once the pills started to kill me on the inside, my outer reality became extremely chaotic. I was starting to manifest my own death unknowingly, and then I started to have accidents happen with a near-death experience that made me step back to really analyze myself and what I was going through on a vibrational level. I went to the extreme to completely cleanse my mind, body, and soul, but that's what it took to bring joy back into my life.

For most of my life, I consumed genetically modified organism (GMO) food and drugs that changed my vibrational frequency. To put it simply, when you're in a low-vibrational energy, you may experience negative thoughts and emotions that come to you in the form of other people carrying these emotions. Once you notice these patters, you will become more consciously aware of your own feelings and mental state. This is when you start to become aware and truly awakened IMO.

Now, Let's go a bit deeper into what was happening in my body through my drug use.

Pain Pills

I opened up a human anatomy book not to long ago and saw that there's a vein an artery that goes to every cell in our body. When I'd swallow a narcotic pill, it would dissolve in my stomach and enter my blood stream and then travel throughout my entire body into every cell affecting my vibration. And in turn, my immune system was weakened. I'd attract viruses or bacteria in the form of people which would make me sick. During my pill-taken days, I was a magnet for illness. If I didn't have my pills, I couldn't get out of bed.

I started to accumulate fat in my belly, and neck. I lost a couple of teeth, and I'd bleed easily because my skin wasn't strong. The "kryptonite" was killing Superman slowly. I was melting like the witch from the Wizard of Oz. The pills also blocked my mind from receiving intuitive messages. They turned my heart cold. I forgot how to love.

Today, I don't even take workout supplements anymore. I look for alternative solutions through nature and food for my pre and post workouts. I'm mindful of what I put in my gas tank. Think of your body as a brand-new car. You want the best for it. You can't put two stroke-gas into a regular gas tank. Your car won't run as smoothly as it should; the engine will eventually start to smoke and backfire, or fart!

I don't know if the prescription pills were made to help people or slowly kill people? There's plenty of data out there that suggests we should ban the manufacturing of these pills. All I can say is that in my experience as a human "test dummy," we should ban pain pills outside of hospital care. These pills were named "pain pills" for a reason. The person using them suffers in tremendous pain if they want to quit. Getting off of them is like fighting off a demon that won't let go without a fight.

Fast Food

I won't sugarcoat it: FAST FOOD = FAST DEATH.

Just like pain pills, fast food is poison. It lowers your vibration. Unfortunately, this food can also be addicting. Some people must have a coffee with cream and sugar from Starbucks in the morning, or a McDonald's breakfast as part of their routine. I used to be one of these people. Once I purified my body though, both my taste buds and my body rejected the food and guided me toward healthier options. Instead of eating fast food, I would find a sit-down restaurant with a better menu, or I would bring my lunch. It was difficult to always make the right choice for lunch. This didn't happen overnight.

I tried to eat a McDonald's breakfast recently, and I paid for it. I had heart burn for almost six hours. I felt like the devil was squeezing my heart with his hand just to torcher me. I must have had a built-up immune system for this type of food during my unhealthy days. I honestly don't know how I could have feed this poison to my kids! I apologize to them in spirit all the time for my lack of knowledge while raising them.

Jesus was a master healer, and spoke the truth about fasting in the Bible. Once I learned how to fast properly, if fast food was the only option, fasting made it easier to hold out until I found a healthier option. When I changed my diet, I changed my life. I wasn't killing myself on the inside anymore. I took my power back and raised my energy. I'm fully focused on whatever I do now. It all started with taking responsibility for my own energy and vibration. I Imagine a world full of energetic people living life to the fullest manifesting their greatest life. Earth would be an even more awesome place.

CHAPTER SEVEN
Tim's Five Day Detox

If your serious about changing your life and stepping back into your power, here's how I purified my body with no pills or supplements. Feel free to use my method or use it as a guide to create one that works for you. To be honest, whenever I read this chapter, I start fasting and eating fruit. With dedication, you will change your vibration for the better. I would recommend that you take time off work so you can focus on your cleanse.

Fortunately, I was able to stumble on the knowledge I have inside of me today through my travels so I could bring my findings to you. When I left for China, I wasn't a small person for my size. I had 38-years of built-up junk in my body. I didn't know I was unhealthy. I always thought I was buff lol. I didn't know my stomach was full of rotting food, and my intestines were full of shit until I went through my purge in China. I didn't know eating fast food, can vegetables, sugar, and processed meat was bad for me. I was raised on it.

Once I started withdrawing from the Norco's, I knew the pills weren't good for me, but I couldn't get off of them without getting sick. Looking back, I had to leave the country. If I didn't, I wouldn't be writing this book.

Over the next five days you'll likely notice a change in the way you feel and look. Your body will start to gravitate away from junk food. You'll cleanse and strengthen the blood flowing through your veins, which will facilitate your healing.

I also suggest incorporating breath-work into your detox, which help relax the body and oxygenate the blood. I use the (Wim-Hof Method), and as Wim says, "Life starts with the breath, and ends with the breath."

Disclaimer: Remember to consult with your doctor before making any changes to your diet, or medication. You can always adjust this method to meet your needs.

Note: Full disclosure, I still went through withdrawals. The toughest part to cleansing your mind, body, and soul is getting started. But anything worth doing requires putting in the work. So roll up your sleeves and let's get started. And, try to have some fun with this!

Day One:

- In the morning, move and stretch your body to get the blood flowing.
- Spend time relaxing in Nature.

- Eat fruits and raw vegetables. Choose those that will fill you up and help you have bowel movement the next day. Some good options include avocados, raw beets, tamarind fruit, beans, citrus, pineapple, and cranberries. Plants are nature's medicine! Don't eat past 6:00 p.m. This is your last meal for day two's fast.
- Throughout the day, drink natural spring water. Listen to your body when it comes to water intake—it will let you know when you have had enough. You don't want to overdo it. Stay away from alcohol, soda, and caffeinated beverages. Drink decaffeinated herbal tea instead of coffee.

Day Two:

- Move and stretch your body.
- Do a twenty-four-hour water fast. Your fast will have started at 6:00 p.m. the previous day. Drink your fill of water. Water fasting allows the body to start flushing itself out. The fruits and vegetables you ate the previous day will help with this.

Tips: I suggest finding an activity to occupy your mind. Go for a long walk or meditate (I love to meditate while fasting; the energy feels stronger). Focus on being in your own presence. If you feel as if you can't fast for the full twenty-four hours, cut up a small beet or sweet potato and eat a handful to quiet your stomach. Sleep if you need to. Try to avoid places where you'll be tempted to eat.

Day Three:

* Move and stretch your body in the morning.
* If you have a blender, make a vegetable smoothie for your first meal of the day. Blend a purple, or regular sweet potato with kale, celery, walnuts or sliced almonds, a banana, honey, raspberries, and blueberries in spring or distilled water. This is actually a powerful drink full of live vegetables. (YUM)! But again, you can change this recipe to fit your diet.
* Throughout the day, eat fruit, vegetables, nuts, or maybe some noodles plates like a vegetable pasta with an olive oil lemon sauce. (NOT Instant noodles). Don't eat too much to compensate for the last two days. Eat your fill and that's it. Don't eat past 6:00 p.m., to prepare for day four's fast.
* Rest and Relax! I gain energy from fasting, but if your doing this for the first time, you'll likely feel tired.

Day Four:

* Move and stretch your body in the morning.
* Do another twenty-four-hour water fast.

Tips: Don't think too much. Go with the flow, Rest, Relax, Mediate, do some Yoga. And don't be surprised if your bowel movements aren't solid. You're cleansing the system.

Day Five:

- Wake up when you feel like it! Drink some water, and have a small bite. Eat a light meal. I suggest that staying away from any heavy, greasy food like cow milk, pancakes, waffles, or bacon. This food will make you feel tired. Oatmeal with fruit would be an ideal breakfast. Try to go as far as you can between your meals from this point forward.
- Stretch your body, and go for a long walk/hike to get the blood moving. In the first four days, you started the process of removing years of built-up toxins in every single cell of your body. Now, you need to get oxygen into the blood and get that circulating. Again, this is why a breathing exercise (I use the Wim Hof Method) or walking each day is an added benefit.

This is only the beginning. Now, you start living a better life!

Once you've finished your initial cleanse, start paying attention to the food you put into your body, and after you eat, take note of how you feel. Listen to your body. It will tell you if the food is good for you or not. If you feel super tired, bloated, or heavy after you eat something, you've likely eaten too much, or the food isn't a match for your body. If you feel energized, happy, and ready for the day, then you're on to something. Keep eating what makes you feel good, and not what simply tastes good!

Start eliminating foods and drinks that were made in a lab with fake ingredients. But cut yourself some slack if you have a bad day and ate some junk food. We all fall back into our default programming sometimes. But if we never teach our kids how to eat right from the start, they will never know.

Conclusion

These days I feel as though I live in heaven on earth. My life is more peaceful than I could ever imagined. I try to meet new people every day for friendly conversations and laughs. I love to laugh these days—I no longer live in darkness. I try to be positive and energetic everywhere I go, even when the people around me don't feel the same way. All I can do is create great experiences for myself and live my life.

I love going to the beach and swimming in the ocean again. I love to cook healthy food for me and others when I get the chance. I love snowboarding again, and this has given me an activity to do with my kids.

Our actions matter. The children in our life watch us. Once we learn how to take care of ourselves, we can teach the next generation how to eat properly and guide them through life with better knowledge than we had growing up to ensure that the next generation will continue to evolve and grow for the better. It's up to us to lead our youth into a life full of great health, love and from there, will come prosperity.

I'm excited for what's to come as I step into my new skin. I have plans on creating wellness destinations around the world. Until then, I need to continue learning and expanding my knowledge. Today, every chance I get to travel, I go! Everything's looking up and love's just around the corner.

When I finally settle down into my new environment, I now have the knowledge I need to achieve whatever my heart desires. The second chapter of my life will be my best chapter. My book isn't finishes yet. There's more adventures to come.

I want you to know how grateful I am that you took the time to read this book. I hope it offered someone hope. I hope it showed you that there's always a light at the end of the tunnel. When your full of energy, you can Create a reality full of love, happiness, laughter, good health, and prosperity. Turn off the TV programming and live your best life, baby!

Conclusion

I'll leave you with some positive affirmations that you can repeat to yourself every day:

I AM love

I AM healthy

I AM strong

I AM a great leader

I AM an amazing person

I attract great people into my life

I AM present

I AM the Universe

"I love to eat clean, drink water, and meditate.
I love to cook, and rest in nature when I need peace"

About the Author

Tim was born in San Bernardino, California. After years of being addicted to pain pills, he learned how to heal himself, purify his body, and raise his vibration. Since then, he's been on a quest to learn as much as possible about nutrition and meditation. He's lived an exciting life full of lessons, and he continues to grow as a person while on earth. *When "Eye" Woke Up* is his first book.

If you would like to support Tim and his fight against opioids, or get in touch with him to speak, you can contact him through email:

Whentimwokeup@gmail.com

or

Tim@1fourwellness.com

Made in the USA
Middletown, DE
05 June 2023

31883927R00073